The New World Order

H. G. Wells

Filiquarian Publishing, LLC

Contents

H. G. Wells

Chapter 1

The End of an Age

In this small book I want to set down as compactly, clearly and usefully as possible the gist of what I have learnt about war and peace in the course of my life. I am not going to write peace propaganda here. I am going to strip down certain general ideas and realities of primary importance to their framework, and so prepare a nucleus of useful knowledge for those who have to go on with this business of making a world peace. I am not going to persuade people to say "Yes, yes" for a world peace; already we have had far too much abolition of war by making declarations and signing resolutions; everybody wants peace or pretends to want peace, and there is no need to add even a sentence more to the vast volume of such ineffective stuff. I am simply attempting to state the things we must do and the price we must pay for world peace if we really intend to achieve it.

Until the Great War, the First World War, I did not bother very much about war and peace. Since then I have almost specialised upon this problem. It is not very easy to recall former states of mind out of which, day by day and year by year, one has grown, but I think that in the decades before 1914 not only I but most of my generation - in the British Empire, America, France and indeed throughout most of the civilised world - thought that war was dying out.

So it seemed to us. It was an agreeable and therefore a readily acceptable idea. We imagined the Franco-German War of 1870-71 and the Russo-Turkish War of 1877-78 were the final conflicts between Great Powers, that now there was a Balance of Power sufficiently stable to make further major warfare impracticable. A Triple Alliance faced a Dual Alliance and neither had much reason for attacking the other. We believed war was shrinking to mere expeditionary affairs on the outskirts of our civilisation, a sort of frontier police business. Habits of tolerant intercourse, it seemed, were being strengthened every year that the peace of the Powers remained unbroken.

There was in deed a mild armament race going on; mild by our present standards of equipment; the armament industry was a growing and enterprising on; but we did not see the full implication of that; we preferred to believe that the increasing general good sense would be strong enough to prevent these multiplying guns from actually going off and hitting anything. And we smiled indulgently at uniforms and parades and army manœuvres. They were the time-honoured toys and regalia of kings and emperors. They were part of the display side of life and would never get to actual destruction and killing. I do not think that exaggerates the easy complacency of, let us say, 1895, forty-five years ago. It was a complacency that lasted with most of us up to 1914. In 1914 hardly anyone in Europe or America below the age of fifty had seen anything of war in his own country.

The world before 1900 seemed to be drifting steadily towards a tacit but practical unification. One could travel without a passport over the larger part of Europe; the Postal Union delivered one's letters uncensored and safely from Chile to

China; money, based essentially on gold, fluctuated only very slightly; and the sprawling British Empire still maintained a tradition of free trade, equal treatment and open-handedness to all comers round and about the planet. In the United States you could go for days and never see a military uniform. Compared with to-day that was, upon the surface at any rate, an age of easy-going safety and good humour. Particularly for the North Americans and the Europeans.

But apart from that steady, ominous growth of the armament industry there were other and deeper forces at work that were preparing trouble. The Foreign Offices of the various sovereign states had not forgotten the competitive traditions of the eighteenth century. The admirals and generals were contemplating with something between hostility and fascination, the hunger weapons the steel industry was gently pressing into their hands. Germany did not share the self-complacency of the English-speaking world; she wanted a place in the sun; there was increasing friction about the partition of the raw material regions of Africa; the British suffered from chronic Russophobia with regard to their vast apportions in the East, and set themselves to nurse Japan into a modernised imperialist power; and also they "remembered Majuba"; the United States were irritated by the disorder of Cuba and felt that the weak, extended Spanish possessions would be all the better for a change of management. So the game of Power Politics went on, but it went on upon the margins of the prevailing peace. There were several wars and changes of boundaries, but they involved no fundamental disturbance of the general civilised life; they did not seem to threaten its broadening tolerations and understandings in any fundamental fashion. Economic stresses and social trouble stirred and muttered beneath the orderly surfaces of political life, but threatened no convulsion. The idea of altogether eliminating war, of clearing what was left of it away, was in the air, but it was free from any sense of urgency. The Hague Tribunal was established and there was a steady dissemination of the conceptions of arbitration and international law. It really seemed to many that the peoples of the earth were settling down in their various territories to a litigious rather than a belligerent order. If there was much social injustice it was being mitigated more and more by a quickening sense of social decency. Acquisitiveness conducted itself with decorum and public-spiritedness was in fashion. Some of it was quite honest public-spiritedness.

In those days, and they are hardly more than half a lifetime behind us, no one thought of any sort of world administration. That patchwork of great Powers and small Powers seemed the most reasonable and practicable method of running the business of mankind. Communications were far too difficult for any sort of centralised world controls. Around the World in Eighty Days, when it was published seventy years ago, seemed an extravagant fantasy. It was a world without telephone or radio, with nothing swifter than a railway train or more destructive than the earlier types of H.E. shell. They were marvels. It was far more convenient to administer that world of the Balance of Power in separate national areas and, since there were such limited facilities for peoples to get at one another and do each other mischiefs, there seemed no harm in ardent patriotism and the complete independence of separate sovereign states.

Economic life was largely directed by irresponsible private businesses and private finance which, because of their private ownership, were able to spread out their unifying transactions in a network that paid little attention to frontiers and national, racial or religious sentimentality. "Business" was much more of a world commonwealth than the political organisations. There were many people, especially in America, who imagined that "Business" might ultimately unify the world and governments sink into subordination to its network.

Nowadays we can be wise after the event and we can see that below this fair surface of things, disruptive forces were steadily gathering strength. But these disruptive forces played a comparatively small rôle in the world spectacle of half a century ago, when the ideas of that older generation which still dominates our political life and the political education of its successors, were formed. It is from the conflict of those Balance of Power and private enterprise ideas, half a century old, that one of the main stresses of our time arises. These ideas worked fairly well in their period and it is still with extreme reluctance that our rulers, teachers, politicians, face the necessity for a profound mental adaptation of their views, methods and interpretations to these disruptive forces that once seemed so negligible and which are now shattering their old order completely.

It was because of this belief in a growing good-will among nations, because of the general satisfaction with things as they were, that the German declarations of war in 1914 aroused such a storm of indignation throughout the entire comfortable world. It was felt that the German Kaiser had broken the tranquillity of the world club, wantonly and needlessly. The war was fought "against the Hohenzollerns." They were to be expelled from the club, certain punitive fines were to be paid and all would be well. That was the British idea of 1914. This out-of-date war business was then to be cleared up once for all by a mutual guarantee by all the more respectable members of the club through a League of Nations. There was no apprehension of any deeper operating causes in that great convulsion on the part of the worthy elder statesmen who made the peace. And so Versailles and its codicils.

For twenty years the disruptive forces have gone on growing beneath the surface of that genteel and shallow settlement, and twenty years there has been no resolute attack upon the riddles with which their growth confronts us. For all that period of the League of Nations has been the opiate of liberal thought in the world.

To-day there is war to get rid of Adolf Hitler, who has now taken the part of the Hohenzollerns in the drama. He too has outraged the Club Rules and he too is to be expelled. The war, the Chamberlain-Hitler War, is being waged so far by the British Empire in quite the old spirit. It has learnt nothing and forgotten nothing. There is the same resolute disregard of any more fundamental problem.

Still the minds of our comfortable and influential ruling-class people refuse to accept the plain intimation that their time is over, that the Balance of Power and uncontrolled business methods cannot continue, and that Hitler, like the Hohenzollerns, is a mere offensive pustule on the face of a deeply ailing world. To get rid of him and his Nazis will be no more a cure for the world's ills than scraping will heal measles. The disease will manifest itself in some new eruption. It is the system of nationalist individualism and unco-ordinated enterprise that is the world's disease, and it is the whole system that has to go. It has to be reconditioned down to its foundations or replaced. It cannot hope to "muddle through" amiably, wastefully and dangerously, a second time.

World peace means all that much revolution. More and more of us begin to realise that it cannot mean less.

The first thing, therefore that has to be done in thinking out the primary problems of world peace is to realise this, that we are living in the end of a definite period of history, the period of the sovereign states. As we used to say in the eighties with ever-increasing truth: "We are in an age of transition". Now we get some measure of the acuteness of the transition. It is a phase of human life which may lead, as I am trying to show, either to a new way of living for our species or else to a longer or briefer dégringolade of violence, misery, destruction, death and the extinction of mankind. These are not rhetorical phrases I am using here; I mean exactly what I say, the disastrous extinction of mankind.

That is the issue before us. It is no small affair of parlour politics we have to consider. As I write, in the moment, thousands of people are being killed, wounded, hunted, tormented, ill-treated, delivered up to the most intolerable and hopeless anxiety and destroyed morally and mentally, and there is nothing in sight at present to arrest this spreading process and prevent its reaching you and yours. It is coming for you and yours now at a great pace. Plainly in so far as we are rational foreseeing creatures there is nothing for any of us now but to make this world peace problem the ruling interest and direction of our lives. If we run away from it it will pursue and get us. We have to face it. We have to solve it or be destroyed by it. It is as urgent and comprehensive as that.

11

H. G. Wells

Chapter 2

Open Conference

Before we examine what I have called so far the "disruptive forces" in the current social order, let me underline one primary necessity for the most outspoken free discussion of the battling organisations and the crumbling institutions amidst which we lead our present uncomfortable and precarious lives. There must be no protection for leaders and organisations from the most searching criticism, on the plea that out country is or may be at war. Or on any pretence. We must talk openly, widely and plainly. The war is incidental; the need for revolutionary reconstruction is fundamental. None of us are clear as yet upon some of the most vital questions before us, we are not lucid enough in our own minds to be ambiguous, and a mumbling tactfulness and indirect half-statements made with an eye upon some censor, will confuse our thoughts and the thoughts of those with whom we desire understanding, to the complete sterilisation and defeat of every reconstructive effort.

We want to talk and tell exactly what our ideas and feelings are, not only to our fellow citizens, but to our allies, to neutrals and, above all, to the people who are marshalled in arms against us. We want to get the same sincerity from them. Because until we have worked out a common basis of ideas with them, peace will be only an uncertain equilibrium while fresh antagonisms develop.

Concurrently with this war we need a great debate. We want
every possible person in the world to take part in that debate. It
is something much more important than the actual warfare. It is
intolerable to think of this storm of universal distress leading
up to nothing but some "conference" of diplomatists out of
touch with the world, with secret sessions, ambiguous
"understandings." . . . Not twice surely can that occur. And yet
what is going to prevent its recurring?

It is quite easy to define the reasonable limits of censorship in a
belligerent country. It is manifest that the publication of any
information likely to be of the slightest use to an enemy must
be drastically anticipated and suppressed; not only direct
information, for example, but intimations and careless
betrayals about the position and movements of ships, troops,
camps, depots of munitions, food supplies, and false reports of
defeats and victories and coming shortages, anything that may
lead to blind panic and hysteria, and so forth and so on. But the
matter takes on a different aspect altogether when it comes to
statements and suggestions that may affect public opinion in
one's own country or abroad, and which may help us towards
wholesome and corrective political action.

One of the more unpleasant aspects of a state of war under
modern conditions is the appearance of a swarm of individuals,
too clever by half, in positions of authority. Excited, conceited,
prepared to lie, distort and generally humbug people into states
of acquiescence, resistance, indignation, vindictiveness, doubt
and mental confusion, states of mind supposed to be
conductive to a final military victory. These people love to
twist and censor facts. It gives them a feeling of power; if they
cannot create they can at least prevent and conceal. Particularly

they poke themselves in between us and the people with whom we are at war to distort any possible reconciliation. They sit, filled with the wine of their transitory powers, aloof from the fatigues and dangers of conflict, pulling imaginary strings in people's minds.

In Germany popular thought is supposed to be under the control of Herr Dr Goebbels; in Great Britain we writers have been invited to place ourselves at the disposal of some Ministry of Information, that is to say at the disposal of hitherto obscure and unrepresentative individuals, and write under its advice. Officials from the British Council and the Conservative Party Headquarters appear in key positions in this Ministry of Information. That curious and little advertised organisation I have just mentioned, the creation I am told of Lord Lloyd, that British Council, sends emissaries abroad, writers, well-dressed women and other cultural personages, to lecture, charm and win over foreign appreciation for British characteristics, for British scenery, British political virtues and so forth. Somehow this is supposed to help something or other. Quietly, unobtrusively, this has gone on. Maybe these sample British give unauthorised assurances but probably they do little positive harm. But they ought not to be employed at all. Any government propaganda is contrary to the essential spirit of democracy. The expression of opinion and collective thought should be outside the range of government activities altogether. It should be the work of free individuals whose prominence is dependent upon the response and support of the general mind.

But here I have to make amends to Lord Lloyd. I was led to believe that the British Council was responsible for Mr. Teeling, the author of Crisis for Christianity, and I said as much in The Fate of Homo Sapiens. I now unsay it. Mr.

15

Teeling, I gather, was sent out upon his journeys by a Catholic newspaper. The British Council was entirely innocent of him.

It is not only that the Ministries of Information and Propaganda do their level best to divert the limited gifts and energies of such writers, lecturers and talkers as we possess, to the production of disingenuous muck that will muddle the public mind and mislead the enquiring foreigner, but that they show a marked disposition to stifle any free and independent utterances that my seem to traverse their own profound and secret plans for the salvation of mankind.

Everywhere now it is difficult to get adequate, far-reaching publicity for outspoken discussion of the way the world is going, and the political, economic and social forces that carry us along. This is not so much due to deliberate suppression as to the general disorder into which human affairs are dissolving. There is indeed in the Atlantic world hardly a sign as yet of that direct espionage upon opinion that obliterates the mental life of the intelligent Italian or German or Russian to-day almost completely; one may still think what one likes, say what one likes and write what one likes, but nevertheless there is already an increasing difficulty in getting bold, unorthodox views heard and read. Newspapers are afraid upon all sorts of minor counts, publishers, with such valiant exceptions as the publishers of this matter, are morbidly discreet; they get Notice D to avoid this or that particular topic; there are obscure boycotts and trade difficulties hindering the wide diffusion of general ideas in countless ways. I do not mean there is any sort of organised conspiracy to suppress discussion, but I do say that the Press, the publishing and bookselling organisations in our free countries, provide a very ill-organised and inadequate machinery for the ventilation and distribution of thought.

Publishers publish for nothing but safe profits; it would astound a bookseller to tell him he was part of the world's educational organisation or a publisher's traveller, that he existed for any other purpose than to book maximum orders for best sellers and earn a record commission - letting the other stuff, the highbrow stuff and all that, go hang. They do not understand that they ought to put public service before gain. They have no inducement to do so and no pride in their function. Theirs is the morale of a profiteering world. Newspapers like to insert brave-looking articles of conventional liberalism, speaking highly of peace and displaying a noble vagueness about its attainment; now we are at war they will publish the fiercest attacks upon the enemy - because such attacks are supposed to keep up the fighting spirit of the country; but any ideas that are really loudly and clearly revolutionary they dare not circulate at all. Under these baffling conditions there is no thorough discussion of the world outlook whatever, anywhere. The democracies are only a shade better than the dictatorships in this respect. It is ridiculous to represent them as realms of light at issue with darkness.

This great debate upon the reconstruction of the world is a thing more important and urgent than the war, and there exist no adequate media for the utterance and criticism and correction of any broad general convictions. There is a certain fruitless and unproductive spluttering of constructive ideas, but there is little sense of sustained enquiry, few real interchanges, inadequate progress, nothing is settled, nothing is dismissed as unsound and nothing is won permanently. No one seems to hear what anyone else is saying. That is because there is no sense of an audience for these ideologists. There is no effective audience saying rudely and obstinately: "What A. has said,

17

seems important. Will B. and C., instead of bombinating in the void, tell us exactly where and why they differ from A.? And now we have got to the common truth of A., B., C., and D. Here is F. saying something. Will he be so good as to correlate what he has to say with A., B., C., and D.?"

But there is no such background of an intelligently observant and critical world audience in evidence. There are a few people here and there reading and thinking in disconnected fragments. This is all the thinking our world is doing in the face of planetary disaster. The universities, bless them! are in uniform or silent.

We need to air our own minds; we need frank exchanges, if we are to achieve any common understanding. We need to work out a clear conception of the world order we would prefer to this present chaos, we need to dissolve or compromise upon our differences so that we may set our faces with assurance towards an attainable world peace. The air is full of the panaceas of half-wits, none listening to the others and most of them trying to silence the others in their impatience. Thousands of fools are ready to write us a complete prescription for our world troubles. Will people never realise their own ignorance and incompleteness, from which arise this absolute necessity for the plainest statement of the realities of the problem, for the most exhaustive and unsparing examination of differences of opinion, and for the most ruthless canvassing of every possibility, however unpalatable it may seem at first, of the situation?

Before anything else, therefore, in this survey of the way to world peace, I put free speech and vigorous publication. It is the thing best worth fighting for. It is the essence of your personal honour. It is your duty as a world citizen to do what you can for that. You have not only to resist suppressions, you have to fight your way out of the fog. If you find your bookseller or newsagent failing to distribute any type of publication whatever - even if you are in entire disagreement with the views of that publication - you should turn the weapon of the boycott upon the offender and find another bookseller or newsagent for everything you read. The would-be world citizen should subscribe also to such organisation as the National Council for Civil Liberties; he should use any advantage his position may give him to check suppression of free speech; and he should accustom himself to challenge nonsense politely but firmly and say fearlessly and as clearly as possible what is in his mind and to listen as fearlessly to whatever is said to him. So that he may know better either through reassurance or correction. To get together with other people to argue and discuss, to think and organise and then implement thought is the first duty of every reasonable man.

This world of ours is going to pieces. It has to be reconstructed and it can only be effectively reconstructed in the light. Only the free, clear, open mind can save us, and these difficulties and obstructions on our line of thought are as evil as children putting obstacles on a railway line or scattering nails on an automobile speed track.

This great world debate must go on, and it must go on now. Now while the guns are still thudding, is the time for thought. It is incredibly foolish to talk as so many people do of ending the war and then having a World Conference to inaugurate a new age. So soon as the fighting stops the real world conference, the live discussion, will stop, too. The diplomats

19

and politicians will assemble with an air of profound competence and close the doors upon the outer world and resume - Versailles. While the silenced world gapes and waits upon their mysteries.

Chapter 3

Disruptive Forces

And now let us come to the disruptive forces that have reduced that late-nineteenth-century dream of a powerful world patchwork of more and more civilised states linked by an ever-increasing financial and economic interdependence, to complete incredibility, and so forced upon every intelligent mind the need to work out a new conception of the World that ought to be. It is supremely important that the nature of these disruptive forces should be clearly understood and kept in mind. To grasp them is to hold the clues to the world's present troubles. To forget about them, even for a moment, is to lose touch with essential reality and drift away into minor issues.

The first group of these forces is what people are accustomed to speak of as "the abolition of distance" and "the change of scale" in human operations. This "abolition of distance" began rather more than a century ago, and its earlier effects were not disruptive at all. It knit together the spreading United States of America over distances that might otherwise have strained their solidarity to the breaking-point, and it enabled the sprawling British Empire to sustain contacts round the whole planet.

The disruptive influence of the abolition of distance appeared only later. Let us be clear upon its essential significance. For what seemed like endless centuries the swiftest means of locomotion had been the horse on the high-road, the running man, the galley and the uncertain, weather-ruled sailing ship. (There was the Dutchman on skates on skates on his canals, but that was an exceptional culmination of speed and not for general application.) The political, social and imaginative life of man for all those centuries was adapted to these limiting conditions. They determined the distances to which marketable goods could conveniently be sent, the limits to which the ruler could send his orders and his solders, the bounds set to getting news, and indeed the whole scale of living. There could be very little real community feeling beyond the range of frequent intercourse.

Human life fell naturally therefore into areas determined by the interplay between these limitations and such natural obstacles as seas and mountains. Such countries as France, England, Egypt, Japan, appeared and reappeared in history like natural, necessary things, and though there were such larger political efforts as the Roman Empire, they never attained an enduring unity. The Roman Empire held together like wet blotting-paper; it was always falling to pieces. The older Empires, beyond their national nuclei, were mere precarious tribute-levying powers. What I have already called the world patchwork of the great and little Powers, was therefore, under the old horse-and-foot and sailing-ship conditions, almost as much a matter of natural necessity as the sizes of trees and animals.

Within a century all this has been changed and we have still to face up to what that change means for us.

First came steam, the steam-railway, the steamship, and then in a quickening crescendo came the internal combustion engine, electrical traction, the motor car, the motor boat, the aeroplane, the transmission of power from central power stations, the telephone, the radio. I feel apologetic in reciting this well-known story. I do so in order to enforce the statement that all the areas that were the most convenient and efficient for the old, time-honoured way of living, became more and more inconveniently close and narrow for the new needs. This applied to every sort of administrative area, from municipalities and urban districts and the range of distributing businesses, up to sovereign states. They were - and for the most part they still are - too small for the new requirements and far too close together. All over the social layout this tightening-up and squeezing together is an inconvenience, but when it comes to the areas of sovereign states it becomes impossibly dangerous. It becomes an intolerable thing; human life cannot go on, with the capitals of most of the civilised countries of the world within an hour's bombing range of their frontiers, behind which attacks can be prepared and secret preparations made without any form of control. And yet we are still tolerant and loyal to arrangements that seek to maintain this state of affairs and treat it as though nothing else were possible.

The present war for and against Hitler and Stalin and Mr. Chamberlain and so forth, does not even touch upon the essential problem of the abolition of distance. It may indeed destroy everything and still settle nothing. If one could wipe out all the issues of the present conflict, we should still be confronted with the essential riddle, which is the abolition of the boundaries of most existing sovereign states and their merger in some larger Pax. We have to do that if any supportable human life is to go on. Treaties and mutual guarantees are not enough. We have surely learnt enough about the value of treaties during the last half-century to realise that.

23

We have, because of the abolition of distance alone, to gather
human affairs together under one common war-preventing
control.

But this abolition of distance is only one most vivid aspect of
the change in the conditions of human life. Interwoven with
that is a general change of scale in human operations. The past
hundred years has been an age of invention and discovery
beyond the achievements of the preceding three millennia. In a
book I published eight years ago, The Work, Wealth and
Happiness of Mankind, I tried to summarise the conquest of
power and substances that is still going on. There is more
power expended in a modern city like Birmingham in a day
than we need to keep the whole of Elizabethan England going
for a year; there is more destructive energy in a single tank than
sufficed the army of William I for the conquest of England.
Man is able now to produce or destroy on a scale beyond
comparison greater than he could before this storm of invention
began. And the consequence is the continual further dislocation
of the orderly social life of our great-great-grandfathers. No
trade, no profession, is exempt. The old social routines and
classifications have been, as people say, "knocked silly". There
is no sort of occupation, fisheries, farming, textile work, metal
work, mining which is not suffering from constant
readjustment to new methods and facilities. Our traditions of
trade and distribution flounder after these changes. Skilled
occupations disappear in the general liquefaction.

The new power organisations are destroying the forests of the
world at headlong speed, ploughing great grazing areas into
deserts, exhausting mineral resources, killing off whales, seals
and a multitude of rare and beautiful species, destroying the
morale of every social type and devastating the planet. The

institutions of the private appropriation of land and natural resources generally, and of private enterprise for profit, which did produce a fairly tolerable, stable and "civilised" social life for all but the most impoverished, in Europe, America and East, for some centuries, have been expanded to a monstrous destructiveness by the new opportunities. The patient, nibbling, enterprising profit-seeker of the past, magnified and equipped now with the huge claws and teeth the change of scale has provided for him, has torn the old economic order to rags. Quite apart from war, our planet is being wasted and disorganised. Yet the process goes on, without any general control, more monstrously destructive even than the continually enhanced terrors of modern warfare.

Now it has to be made clear that these two things, the manifest necessity for some collective world control to eliminate warfare and the less generally admitted necessity for a collective control of the economic and biological life of mankind, are aspects of one and the same process. Of the two the disorganisation of the ordinary life which is going on, war or no war, is the graver and least reversible. Both arise out of the abolition of distance and the change of scale, they affect and modify each other, and unless their parallelism and interdependence are recognised, any projects for world federation or anything of the sort are doomed inevitably to frustration.

That is where the League of nations broke down completely. It was legal; it was political. It was devised by an ex-professor of the old-fashioned history assisted by a few politicians. It ignored the vast disorganisation of human life by technical revolutions, big business and modern finance that was going on, of which the Great War itself was scarcely more than a by-product. It was constituted as though nothing of that sort was occurring.

This war storm which is breaking upon us now, due to the continued fragmentation of human government among a patchwork of sovereign states, is only one aspect of the general need for a rational consolidation of human affairs. The independent sovereign state with its perpetual war threat, armed with the resources of modern mechanical frightfulness, is only the most blatant and terrifying aspect of that same want of a coherent general control that makes overgrown, independent, sovereign, private business organisations and combinations, socially destructive. We should still be at the mercy of the "Napoleons" of commerce and the "Attilas" of finance, if there was not a gun or a battleship or a tank or a military uniform in the world. We should still be sold up and dispossessed.

Political federation, we have to realise, without a concurrent economic collectivisation, is bound to fail. The task of the peace-maker who really desires peace in a new world, involves not merely a political but a profound social revolution, profounder even than the revolution attempted by the Communists in Russia. The Russian Revolution failed not by its extremism but through the impatience, violence and intolerance of its onset, through lack of foresight and intellectual insufficiency. The cosmopolitan revolution to a world collectivism, which is the only alternative to chaos and degeneration before mankind, has to go much further than the Russian; it has to be more thorough and better conceived and its achievement demands a much more heroic and more steadfast thrust.

It serves no useful purpose to shut our eyes to the magnitude and intricacy of the task of making the world peace. These are the basic factors of the case.

H. G. Wells

Chapter 4

Class-War

Now here it is necessary to make a distinction which is far too frequently ignored. Collectivisation means the handling of the common affairs of mankind by a common control responsible to the whole community. It means the suppression of go-as-you-please in social and economic affairs just as much as in international affairs. It means the frank abolition of profit-seeking and of every devise by which human+beings contrive to be parasitic on their fellow man. It is the practical realisation of the brotherhood of man through a common control. It means all that and it means no more than that.

The necessary nature of that control, the way to attain it and to maintain it have still to be discussed.

The early forms of socialism were attempts to think out and try out collectivist systems. But with the advent of Marxism, the larger idea of collectivism became entangled with a smaller one, the perpetual conflict of people in any unregulated social system to get the better of one another. Throughout the ages this has been going on. The rich, the powerful generally, the more intelligent and acquisitive have got away with things, and sweated, oppressed, enslaved, bought and frustrated the less intelligent, the less acquisitive and the unwary. The Haves in every generation have always got the better of the Have-nots,

29

and the Have-nots have always resented the privations of their disadvantage.

So it is and so in the uncollectivised world it has always been. The bitter cry of the expropriated man echoes down the ages from ancient Egypt and the Hebrew prophets, denouncing those who grind the faces of the poor. At times the Have-nots have been so uneducated, so helplessly distributed among their more successful fellows that they have been incapable of social disturbance, but whenever such developments as plantation of factory labour, the accumulation of men in seaport towns, the disbanding of armies, famine and so forth, brought together masses of men at the same disadvantage, their individual resentments flowed together and became a common resentment. The miseries underlying human society were revealed. The Haves found themselves assailed by resentful, vindictive revolt.

Let us note that these revolts of the Have-nots throughout the ages have sometimes been very destructive, but that invariably they have failed to make any fundamental change in this old, old story of getting and not getting the upper hand. Sometimes the Have-nots have frightened or otherwise moved the Haves to more decent behaviour. Often the Have-nots have found a Champion who has ridden to power on their wrongs. Then the ricks were burnt or the châteaux. The aristocrats were guillotined and their heads carried on exemplary pikes. Such storms passed and when they passed, there for all practical purposes was the old order returning again; new people but the old inequalities. Returning inevitably, with only slight variations in appearance and phraseology, under the condition of a non-collective social order.

The point to note is that in the unplanned scramble of human life through the centuries of the horse-and-foot period, these incessantly recurring outbreaks of the losers against the winners have never once produced any permanent amelioration of the common lot, or greatly changed the features of the human community. Not once.

The Have-nots have never produced the intelligence and the ability and the Haves have never produced the conscience, to make a permanent alteration of the rules of the game. Slave revolts, peasant revolts, revolts of the proletariat have always been fits of rage, acute social fevers which have passed. The fact remains that history produces no reason for supposing that the Have-nots, considered as a whole, have available any reserves of directive and administrative capacity and disinterested devotion, superior to that of the more successful classes. Morally, intellectually, there is no reason to suppose them better.

Many potentially able people may miss education and opportunity; they may not be inherently inferior but nevertheless they are crippled and incapacitated and kept down. They are spoilt. Many specially gifted people may fail to "make good" in a jostling, competitive, acquisitive world and so fall into poverty and into the baffled, limited ways of living of the commonalty, but they too are exceptions. The idea of a right-minded Proletariat ready to take things over is a dream.

As the collectivist idea has developed out of the original propositions of socialism, the more lucid thinkers have put this age-long bitterness of the Haves and the Have-nots into its proper place as part, as the most distressing part, but still only as part, of the vast wastage of human resources that their disorderly exploitation entailed. In the light of current events they have come to realise more and more clearly that the need and possibility of arresting this waste by a world-wide collectivisation is becoming continually more possible and at the same time imperative. They have had no delusions about the education and liberation that is necessary to gain that end. They have been moved less by moral impulses and sentimental pity and so forth, admirable but futile motives, as by the intense intellectual irritation of living in a foolish and destructive system. They are revolutionaries not because the present way of living is a hard and tyrannous way of living, but because it is from top to bottom exasperatingly stupid.

But thrusting athwart the socialist movement towards collectivisation and its research for some competent directive organisation of the world's affairs, came the clumsy initiative of Marxism with its class-war dogma, which has done more to misdirect and sterilise human good-will than any other misconception of reality that has ever stultified human effort.

Marx saw the world from a study and through the hazes of a vast ambition. He swam in the current ideologies of his time and so he shared the prevalent socialist drive towards collectivisation. But while his sounder-minded contemporaries were studying means and ends he jumped from a very imperfect understanding of the Trades Union movement in Britain to the wildest generalisations about the social process. He invented and antagonised two phantoms. One was the Capitalist System; the other the Worker.

There never has been anything on earth that could be properly called a Capitalist System. What was the matter with his world was manifestly its entire want of system. What the Socialists were feeling their way towards was the discovery and establishment of a world system.

The Haves of our period were and are a fantastic miscellany of people, inheriting or getting their power and influence by the most various of the interbreeding social solidarity even of a feudal aristocracy or an Indian caste. But Marx, looking rather into his inner consciousness than at any concrete reality, evolved that monster "System" on his Right. Then over against it, still gazing into that vacuum, he discovered on the Left the proletarians being steadily expropriated and becoming class-conscious. They were just as endlessly various in reality as the people at the top of the scramble; in reality but not in the mind of the Communist seer. There they consolidated rapidly.

So while other men toiled at this gigantic problem of collectivisation, Marx found his almost childlishy simple recipe. All you had to do was to tell the workers that they were being robbed and enslaved by this wicked "Capitalist System" devised by the "bourgeoisie". They need only "unite"; they had "nothing to lose but their chains". The wicked Capitalist System was to be overthrown, with a certain vindictive liquidation of "capitalists" in general and the "bourgeoisie" in particular, and a millennium would ensue under a purely workers' control, which Lenin later on was to crystallise into a phrase of supra-theological mystery, "the dictatorship of the proletariat". The proletarians need learn nothing, plan nothing; they were right and good by nature; they would just "take over". The infinitely various envies, hatreds and resentments of the Have-nots were to fuse into a mighty creative drive. All virtue resided in them; all evil in those who had bettered them. One good thing there was in this new doctrine of the class war, it inculcated a much needed brotherliness among the workers,

33

but it was balanced by the organisation of class hate. So the great propaganda of the class war, with these monstrous falsifications of manifest fact, went forth. Collectivisation would not so much be organised as appear magically when the incubus of Capitalism and all those irritatingly well-to-do people, were lifted off the great Proletarian soul.

Marx was a man incapable in money matters and much bothered by tradesmen's bills. Moreover he cherished absurd pretensions to aristocracy. The consequence was that he romanced about the lovely life of the Middle Ages as if he were another Belloc and concentrated his animus about the "bourgeoisie", whom he made responsible for all those great disruptive forces in human society that we have considered. Lord Bacon, the Marquis of Worcester, Charles the Second and the Royal Society, people like Cavendish and Joule and Watt for example, all became "bourgeoisie" in his inflamed imagination. "During its reign of scarce a century", he wrote in the Communist Manifesto, "the bourgeoisie has created more powerful, more stupendous forces of production than all preceding generations rolled into one . . . . What earlier generations had the remotest inkling that such productive forces slumbered within the wombs of associated labour?"

"The wombs of associated labour!" (Golly, what a phrase!) The industrial revolution which was a consequence of the mechanical revolution is treated as the cause of it. Could facts be muddled more completely?

And again: " . . . the bourgeois system is no longer able to cope with the abundance of wealth it creates. How does the bourgeoisie overcome these crises? On the one hand, by the compulsory annihilation of a quantity of the productive forces;

on the other, by the conquest of new markets and the more thorough exploitation of old ones. With what results? The results are that the way is paved for more widespread and more disastrous crises and that the capacity for averting such crises is lessened.

"The weapons" (Weapons! How that sedentary gentleman in his vast beard adored military images!) "with which the bourgeoisie overthrew feudalism are now being turned against the bourgeoisie itself.

"But the bourgeoisie has not only forged the weapons that will slay it; it has also engendered the men who will use these weapons - the modern workers, the proletarians."

And so here they are, hammer and sickle in hand, chest stuck out, proud, magnificent, commanding, in the Manifesto. But go and look for them yourself in the streets. Go and look at them in Russia.

Even for 1848 this is not intelligent social analysis. It is the outpouring of a man with a B in his bonnet, the hated Bourgeoisie, a man with a certain vision, uncritical of his own sub-conscious prejudices, but shrewd enough to realise how great a driving force is hate and the inferiority complex. Shrewd enough to use hate and bitter enough to hate. Let anyone read over that Communist Manifesto and consider who might have shared the hate or even have got it all, if Marx had not been the son of a rabbi. Read Jews for Bourgeoisie and the Manifesto is pure Nazi teaching of the 1933-8 vintage.

Stripped down to its core in this fashion, the primary falsity of the Marxist assumption is evident. But it is one of the queer

35

common weakness of the human mind to be uncritical of primary assumptions and to smother up any enquiry into their soundness in secondary elaboration, in technicalities and conventional formulæ. Most of our systems of belief rest upon rotten foundations, and generally these foundations are made sacred to preserve them from attack. They become dogmas in a sort of holy of holies. It is shockingly uncivil to say "But that is nonsense". The defenders of all the dogmatic religions fly into rage and indignation when one touches on the absurdity of their foundations. Especially if one laughs. That is blasphemy.

This avoidance of fundamental criticism is one of the greatest dangers to any general human understanding. Marxism is no exception to the universal tendency. The Capitalist System has to be a real system, the Bourgeoisie an organised conspiracy against the Workers, and every human conflict everywhere has to be an aspect of the Class War, or they cannot talk to you. They will not listen to you. Never once has there been an attempt to answer the plain things I have been saying about them for a third of a century. Anything not in their language flows off their minds like water off a duck's back. Even Lenin - by far the subtlest mind in the Communist story - has not escaped this pitfall, and when I talked to him in Moscow in 1920 he seemed quite unable to realise that the violent conflict going on in Ireland between the Catholic nationalists and the Protestant garrison was not his sacred insurrection of the Proletariat in full blast.

To-day there is quite a number of writers, and among them there are men of science who ought to think better, solemnly elaborating a pseudo-philosophy of science and society upon the deeply buried but entirely nonsensical foundations laid by Marx. Month by month the industrious Left book Club pours a

new volume over the minds of its devotees to sustain their
mental habits and pickle them against the septic influence of
unorthodox literature. A party Index of Forbidden Books will
no doubt follow. Distinguished professors with solemn delight
in their own remarkable ingenuity, lecture and discourse and
even produce serious-looking volumes, upon the superiority of
Marxist physics and Marxist research, to the unbranded
activities of the human mind. One tries not to be rude to them,
but it is hard to believe they are not deliberately playing the
fool with their brains. Or have they a feeling that revolutionary
communism is ahead, and are they doing their best to
rationalise it with an eye to those red days to come? (See
Hogben's Dangerous Thoughts.)

Here I cannot pursue in any detail the story of the Rise and
Corruption of Marxism in Russia. It confirms in every
particular my contention that the class-war idea is an
entanglement and perversion of the world drive towards a
world collectivism, a wasting disease of cosmopolitan
socialism. It has followed in its general outline the common
history of every revolt of the Have-nots since history began.
Russia in the shadows displayed an immense inefficiency and
sank slowly to Russia in the dark. Its galaxy of incompetent
foremen, managers, organisers and so forth, developed the
most complicated system of self-protection against criticism,
they sabotaged one another, they intrigued against one another.
You can read the quintessence of the thing in Littlepage's In
Search of Soviet Gold. And like every other Have-not revolt
since the dawn of history, hero worship took possession of the
insurgent masses. The inevitable Champion appeared. They
escape from the Czar and in twenty years they are worshipping
Stalin, originally a fairly honest, unoriginal, ambitious
revolutionary, driven to self-defensive cruelty and inflated by

37

flattery to his present quasi-divine autocracy. The cycle completes itself and we see that like every other merely insurrectionary revolution, nothing has changed; a lot of people have been liquidated and a lot of other people have replaced them and Russia seems returning back to the point at which it started, to a patriotic absolutism of doubtful efficiency and vague, incalculable aims. Stalin, I believe, is honest and benevolent in intention, he believes in collectivism simply and plainly, he is still under the impression that he is making a good thing of Russia and of the countries within her sphere of influence, and he is self-righteously impatient of criticism or opposition. His successor may not have the same disinterestedness.

But I have written enough to make it clear why we have to dissociate collectivisation altogether from the class war in our minds. Let us waste no more time on the spectacle of the Marxist putting the cart in front of the horse and tying himself up with the harness. We have to put all this proletarian distortion of the case out of our minds and start afresh upon the problem of how to realise the new and unprecedented possibilities of world collectivisation that have opened out upon the world in the past hundred years. That is a new story. An entirely different story.

We human+beings are facing gigantic forces that will either destroy our species altogether or lift it to an altogether unprecedented level of power and well-being. These forces have to be controlled or we shall be annihilated. But completely controlled they can abolish slavery - by the one sure means of making these things unnecessary. Class-war communism has its opportunity to realise all this, and it has failed to make good. So far it has only replaced one autocratic

Russia by another. Russia, like all the rest of the world, is still facing the problem of the competent government of a collective system. She has not solved it.

The dictatorship of the proletariat has failed us. We have to look for possibilities of control in other directions. Are they to be found?

NOTE

A friendly adviser reading the passage protests against "the wombs of associated labour" as a mistranslation of the original German of the Manifesto. I took it from the translation of Professor Hirendranath Mukherjee in an Indian students' journal, Sriharsha, which happened to be at my desk. But my adviser produces Lily G. Aitken and Frank C. Budgen in a Glasgow Socialist Labour Press publication, who gave it as "the lap of social labour", which is more refined but pure nonsense. The German word is "schoss", and in its widest sense it means the whole productive maternal outfit from bosom to knees and here quite definitely the womb. The French translation gives "sein", which at the first glance seems to carry gentility to an even higher level. But as you can say in French that an expectant mother carries her child in her "sein", I think Professor Mukherjee has it. Thousands of reverent young Communists must have read that "lap" without observing its absurdity. Marx is trying to make out that the increase of productive efficiency was due to "association" in factories. A better phrase to express his (wrong-headed) intention would have been "the co-ordinated operations of workers massed in factories".

H. G. Wells

Chapter 5

Unsalted Youth

We have now to examine these disruptive forces a little more closely, these disruptive forces which are manifestly overstraining and destroying the social and political system in which most of us have been reared. At what particular points in our political and social life are these disruptive forces discovering breaking-points?

Chief among these breaking-points, people are beginning to realise more and more clearly, is the common, half-educated young man.

One particular consequence of the onrush of power and invention in our time, is the release of a great flood of human energy in the form of unemployed young people. This is a primary factor of the general political instability.

We have to recognise that humanity is not suffering, as most animal species when they suffer to do, from hunger or want in any material form. It is threatened not by deficiency but by excess. It is plethoric. It is not lying down to die through physical exhaustion; it is knocking itself to pieces.

Measured by any standards except human contentment and ultimate security, mankind appears to be much wealthier now than in 1918. The qualities of power and material immediately available are much greater. What is called productivity in general is greater. But there is sound reason for supposing that a large part of this increased productivity is really a swifter and more thorough exploitation of irreplaceable capital. It is a process that cannot go on indefinitely. It rises to a maximum and then the feast is over. Natural resources are being exhausted at a great rate, and the increased output goes into war munitions whose purpose is destruction, and into sterile indulgences no better than waste. Man, "heir of the ages", is a demoralised spendthrift, in a state of galloping consumption, living on stimulants.

When we look into the statistics of population, there is irrefutable proof that everywhere we are passing a maximum (see for this Enid Charles' The Twilight of Parenthood, or R. R. Kuczynski's Measurement of Population Growth) and that a rapid decline is certain not only in Western Europe bur throughout the world. There is sound reason for doubting the alleged vast increase of the Russian people (see Souvarine's Stalin). Nevertheless, because of the continually increasing efficiency of productive methods, the relative pressure of this new unemployed class increases. The "mob" of the twentieth century is quite different from the almost animal "mob" of the eighteenth century. It is a restless sea of dissatisfied young people, of young men who can find no outlet for their natural urgencies and ambitions, young people quite ready to "make trouble" as soon as they are shown how.

In the technically crude past, the illiterate Have-nots were sweated and overworked. It was easy to find toil to keep them all busy. Such surplus multitudes are wanted no more. Toil is no longer marketable. Machines can toil better and with less resistance.

These frustrated multitudes have been made acutely aware of their own frustration. The gap of their always partly artificial disadvantage has been greatly diminished because now they all read. Even for incidental employment it has been necessary to teach them that, and the new reading public thus created has evoked a press and literature of excitement and suggestion. The cinema and the radio dazzle them with spectacles of luxury and unrestricted living. They are not the helpless Hodges and factory fodder of a hundred years ago. They are educated up to what must have been the middle-class level in 1889. They are indeed largely a squeezed-out middle class, restless, impatient and as we shall see extremely dangerous. They have assimilated almost all of the lower strata that were formerly illiterate drudges.

And this modernised excess population has no longer any social humility. It has no belief in the infallible wisdom of its rulers. It sees them too clearly; it knows about them, their waste, vices and weaknesses, with an even exaggerated vividness. It sees no reason for its exclusion from the good things of life by such people. It has lost enough of its inferiority to realise that most of that inferiority is arbitrary and artificial.

You may say that this is a temporary state of affairs, that the fall in population will presently relieve the situation, by getting rid of this surplus of the "not wanted". But it will do nothing of the sort. As population falls, consumption will fall. Industries will still be producing more and more efficiently for a shrinking market and they will be employing fewer and fewer hands. A state of five million people with half a million of useless hands, will be twice as unstable as forty million with two million standing off. So long as the present state of affairs continues, this stratum of perplexed young people "out of it" will increase relatively to the total community.

It is still not realised as clearly as it should be, how much the troubles of the present time are due to this new aspect of the social puzzle. But if you will scrutinise the events of the past half century in the light of this idea, you will see more and more convincingly that it is mainly through this growing mass of unfulfilled desire that the disruptive forces manifest themselves.

The eager and adventurous unemployed young are indeed the shock troops in the destruction of the old social order everywhere. They find guidance in some confident Party or some inspired Champion, who organises them for revolutionary or counter-revolutionary ends. It scarcely matters which. They become Communists or they become Fascists, Nazis, the Irish Republican Army, Ku Klux Klansmen and so forth and so on. The essence is the combination of energy, frustration and discontent. What all such movements have in common, is a genuine indignation at the social institutions that have begotten and then cold-shouldered them, a quasi-military organisation and the resolve to seize power for themselves embodied in their leaders. A wise and powerful government would at any cost anticipate and avert these destructive activities by providing various and interesting new employment and the necessary condition for a satisfying successful life for everyone. These young people are life. The rise of the successful leader only puts off the trouble for a time. He seizes power in the name of his movement. And then?

When the seizure of power has been effected, he finds himself obliged to keep things going, to create justification for his leadership, exciting enterprises, urgencies.

A leader of vision with adequate technical assistance might conceivedly direct much of the human energy he has embodied into creative channels. For example he could rebuild the dirty, inadequate cities of our age, turn the still slovenly country-side into a garden and play-ground, re-clothe, liberate and stimulate imaginations, until the ideas of creative progress became a habit of mind. But in doing this he will find himself confronted by those who are sustained by the pre-emptions and appropriations of the old order. These relatively well-off people will bargain with him up to the last moment for their money and impede his seizure and utilisation of land and material resources, and will be further hampered by the fact that in organising his young people he has had to turn their minds and capacities from creative work to systematic violence and militant activities. It is easy to make an unemployed young man into a Fascist or gangster, but it is hard to turn him back to any decent social task. Moreover the Champion's own leadership was largely due to his conspiratorial and adventurous quality. He is himself unfit for a creative job. He finds himself a fighter at the head of a fighting pack.

And furthermore, unless his country is on the scale of Russia and the United States, whatever he attempts in order to make good his promises of an abundant life, has to be done in face of that mutual pressure of the sovereign states due to the abolition of distance and change of scale which we have already considered. He has no elbow-room in which to operate. The resultant of these convergent difficulties is to turn him and his fighting pack releasing flux of predatory war.

Everywhere in the world, under varying local circumstances, we see governments primarily concerned with this supreme problem of what to do with these young adults who are unemployable under present conditions. We have to realise that and bear it constantly in mind. It is there in every country. It is the most dangerous and wrong-headed view of the world situation, to treat the totalitarian countries as differing fundamentally from the rest of the world.

The problem of reabsorbing the unemployable adult is the essential problem in all states. It is the common shape to which all current political dramas reduce. How are we to use up or slake this surplus of human energy? The young are the live core of our species. The generation below sixteen or seventeen has not yet begun to give trouble, and after forty, the ebb of vitality disposes men to accept the lot that has fallen to them.

Franklin Roosevelt and Stalin find themselves in control of vast countries under-developed or so misdeveloped that their main energies go into internal organisation or reorganisation. They do not press against their frontiers therefore and they do not threaten war. The recent Russian annexations have been precautionary-defensive. But all the same both Russia and America have to cater for that troublesome social stratum quite as much as Europe. The New Deal is plainly an attempt to achieve a working socialism and avert a social collapse in America; it is extraordinarily parallel to the successive "policies" and "Plans" of the Russian experiment. Americans shirk the word "socialism", but what else can one call it?

The British oligarchy, demoralised and slack with the accumulated wealth of a century of advantage, bought off social upheaval for a time by the deliberate and socially demoralising appeasement of the dole. It has made no adequate effort to employ or educate these surplus people; it has just pushed the dole at them. It even tries to buy off the leader of the Labour Party with a salary of £2000 a year. Whatever we may think of the quality and deeds of the Nazi or Fascist regimes or the follies of their leaders, we must at any rate concede that they attempt, however clumsily, to reconstruct life in a collectivist direction. They are efforts to adjust and construct and so far they are in advance of the British ruling class. The British Empire has shown itself the least constructive of all governing networks. It produces no New Deals, no Five Year Plans; it keeps on trying to stave off its inevitable dissolution and carry on upon the old lines - and apparently it will do that until it has nothing more to give away.

"Peace in our time", that foolishly premature self-congratulation of Mr Chamberlain, is manifestly the guiding principle of the British elder statesman. It is that natural desire we all begin to feel after sixty to sit down comfortably somewhere. Unprogressive tranquillity they want at any price, even at the price of a preventive war. This astonishing bunch of rulers has never revealed any conception whatever of a common future before its sprawling Empire. There was a time when that Empire seemed likely to become the nexus of a world system, but now manifestly it has no future but disintegration. Apparently its rulers expected it to go on just as it was for ever. Bit by bit its component parts have dropped away and become quasi-independent powers, generally after an

47

unedifying struggle; Southern Ireland for example is neutral in the present war, South Africa hesitated.

Now, and that is why this book is being written, these people, by a string of almost incredible blunders, have entangled what is left of their Empire in a great war to "end Hitler", and they have absolutely no suggestion to offer their antagonists and the world at large, of what is to come after Hitler. Apparently they hope to paralyse Germany in some as yet unspecified fashion and then to go back to their golf links or the fishing stream and doze by the fire after dinner. That is surely one of the most astounding things in history, the possibility of death and destruction beyond all reckoning and our combatant governments have no idea of what is to follow when the overthrow of Hitler is accomplished. They seem to be as void of any sense of the future, as completely empty-headed about the aftermath of their campaigns, as one of those American Tories who are "just out against F.D.R. Damn him!"

So the British Empire remains, paying its way down to ultimate bankruptcy, buying itself a respite from the perplexing problems of the future, with the accumulated wealth and power of its past. It is rapidly becoming the most backward political organisation in the world. But sooner or later it will have no more money for the dole and no more allies to abandon nor dominions to yield up to their local bosses, and then possibly its disintegration will be complete (R.I.P.), leaving intelligent English people to line up at last with America and the rest of the intelligent world and face the universal problem. Which is: how are we to adapt ourselves to these mighty disruptive forces that are shattering human society as it is at present constituted?

In the compressed countries which have little internal scope and lack the vast natural resources of the Russian and Atlantic communities, the internal tension makes more directly for aggressive warfare, but the fundamental driving-force behind their aggressiveness is still the universal trouble, that surplus of young men.

Seen in this broader vision, the present war falls into its true proportions as a stupid conflict upon secondary issues, which is delaying and preventing an overdue world adjustment. That is may kill hundreds of thousands of people does not alter that. An idiot with a revolver can murder a family. He remains an idiot.

From 1914 to 1939 has been a quarter of a century of folly, meanness, evasion and resentment, and only a very tedious and copious historian would attempt to distribute the blame among those who had played a part in the story. And when he had done it, what he had done would not matter in the least. An almost overwhelmingly difficult problem has confronted us all, and in some measure we have all of us lost our heads in the face of it, lost our dignity, been too clever by half, pinned ourselves to cheap solutions, quarrelled stupidly among ourselves. "We have erred and strayed . . . . We have lest undone those things that we ought to have done and we have done those things which we ought not to have done and there is no health in us."

I do not see any way to a solution of the problem of World Peace unless we begin with a confession of universal wrong-thinking and wrong-doing. Then we can sit down to the question of a solution with some reasonable prospect of finding an answer.

Now let us assume that "we" are a number of intelligent men,
German, French, English, American, Italian, Chinese and so
forth, who have decided in consequence of the war and in spite
of the war, while the war is still going on, to wipe out all these
squabbling bygones from our minds, and discuss plainly and
simply the present situation of mankind. What is to be done
with the world? Let us recapitulate the considerations that so
far have been brought in, and what prospects they open, if any,
of some hopeful concerted action, action that would so
revolutionise the human outlook as to end war and that hectic
recurrent waste of human life and happiness, for ever.

Firstly then it has been made apparent that humanity is at the
end of an age, an age of fragmentation in the management of
its affairs, fragmentation politically among separate sovereign
states and economically among unrestricted business of
organisations competing for profit. The abolition of distance,
the enormous increase of available power, root causes of all
our troubles, have suddenly made what was once a tolerable
working system - a system that was perhaps with all its
inequalities and injustices the only practicable working system
in its time - enormously dangerous and wasteful, so that it
threatens to exhaust and destroy our world altogether. Man is
like a feckless heir who has suddenly been able to get at his
capital and spend it as though it were income. We are living in
a phase of violent and irreparable expenditure. There is an
intensified scramble among nations and among individuals to
acquire, monopolise and spend. The dispossessed young find
themselves hopeless unless they resort to violence. They
implement the ever-increasing instability. Only a
comprehensive collectivisation of human affairs can arrest this

disorderly self-destruction of mankind. All this has been made plain in what has gone before.

This essential problem, the problem of collectivisation, can be viewed from two reciprocal points of view and stated in two different ways. We can ask, "What is to be done to end the world chaos?" and also "How can we offer the common young man a reasonable and stimulating prospect of a full life?"

These two questions are the obverse and reverse of one question. What answers one answers the other. The answer to both is that we have to collectivise the world as one system with practically everyone playing a reasonably satisfying part in it. For sound practical reasons, over and above any ethical or sentimental considerations, we have to devise a collectivisation that neither degrades nor enslaves.

Our imaginary world conference then has to turn itself to the question of how to collectivise the world, so that it will remain collectivised and yet enterprising, interesting and happy enough to content that common young man who will otherwise reappear, baffled and sullen, at the street corners and throw it into confusion again. To that problem the rest of this book will address itself.

As a matter of fact it is very obvious that at the present time a sort of collectivisation is being imposed very rapidly upon the world. Everyone is being enrolled, ordered about, put under control somewhere - even if it is only in an evacuation or concentration camp or what not. This process of collectivisation, collectivisation of some sort, seems now to be in the nature of things and there is no reason to suppose it is reversible. Some people imagine world peace as the end of that process. Collectivisation is going to be defeated and a vaguely conceived reign of law will restore and sustain property, Christianity, individualism and everything to which the respectable prosperous are accustomed. This is implicit even on the title of such a book as Edward Mousley's Man or Leviathan? It is much more reasonable to think that world peace has to be the necessary completion of that process, and that the alternative is a decadent anarchy. If so, the phrase for the aims of liberal thought should be no Man or Leviathan but Man masters Leviathan.

On this point, the inevitability of collectivisation as the sole alternative to universal brigandage and social collapse, our world conference must make itself perfectly clear.

Then it has to turn itself to the much more difficult and complicated question of how.

Chapter 6

Socialism Unavoidable

Let us, even at the cost of a certain repetition, look a little more closely now into the fashion in which the disruptive forces are manifesting themselves in the Western and Eastern hemispheres.

In the Old World the hypertrophy of armies is most conspicuous, in America it was the hypertrophy of big business. But in both the necessity for an increasing collective restraint upon uncoordinated over-powerful business or political enterprise is more and more clearly recognised.

There is a strong opposition on the part of great interests in America to the President, who has made himself the spear-head of the collectivising drive; they want to put the brake now on his progressive socialisation of the nation, and quite possibly, at the cost of increasing social friction, they may slow down the drift to socialism very considerably. But it is unbelievable that they dare provoke the social convulsion that would ensue upon a deliberate reversal of the engines or upon any attempt to return to the glorious days of big business, wild speculation and mounting unemployment before 1927. They will merely slow down the drive. For in the world now all roads lead to socialism or social dissolution.

53

The tempo of the process is different in the two continents; that is the main difference between them. It is not an opposition. They travel at different rates but they travel towards an identical goal. In the Old World at present the socialisation of the community is going on far more rapidly and thoroughly than it is in America because of the perpetual war threat.

In Western Europe now the dissolution and the drive towards socialisation progress by leaps and bounds. The British governing class and British politicians generally, overtaken by a war they had not the intelligence to avert, have tried to atone for their slovenly unimaginativeness during the past twenty years in a passion of witless improvisation. God knows what their actual war preparations amount to, but their domestic policy seems to be based on an imperfect study of Barcelona, Guernica, Madrid and Warsaw. They imagine similar catastrophes on a larger scale - although they are quite impossible, as every steady-headed person who can estimate the available supplies of petrol knows - and they have a terrible dread of being held responsible. They fear a day of reckoning with their long-bamboozled lower classes. In their panic they are rapidly breaking up the existing order altogether.

The changes that have occurred in Great Britain in less than a year are astounding. They recall in many particulars the social dislocation of Russia in the closing months of 1917. There has been a shifting and mixing-up of people that would have seemed impossible to anyone in 1937. The evacuation of centres of population under the mere exaggerated threat of air raids has been of frantic recklessness. Hundreds of thousands of families have been broken up, children separated from their parents and quartered in the homes of more or less reluctant hosts. Parasites and skin diseases, vicious habits and insanitary practices have been spread, as if in a passion of equalitarian propaganda, the slums of such centres as Glasgow, London and Liverpool, throughout the length and breadth of the land. Railways, road traffic, all the normal communications have been dislocated by a universal running about. For a couple of months Great Britain has been more like a disturbed ant-hill than an organised civilised country.

The contagion of funk has affected everyone. Public institutions and great business concerns have bolted to remote and inconvenient sites; the BBC organisation, for example, scuffled off headlong from London, needlessly and ridiculously, no man pursuing it. There has been a wild epidemic of dismissals, of servants employed in London, for example, and a still wilder shifting of unsuitable men to novel, unnecessary jobs. Everyone has been exhorted to serve the country, children of twelve, to the great delight of conservative-minded farmers, have been withdrawn from school and put to work on the land, and yet the number of those who have lost their jobs and cannot find anything else to do, has gone up by over 100,000.

There have been amateurish attempts to ration food, producing waste here and artificial scarcity there. A sort of massacre of small independent businesses is in progress mainly to the advantage of the big provision-dealing concerns, who changed in a night from open profiteers to become the "expert" advisers of food supply. All the expertise they have ever displayed has been the extraction of profits from food supply. But while profits mount, taxation with an air of great resolution sets itself to prune them.

H. G. Wells

The British public has always been phlegmatic in the face of danger, it is too stout-hearted and too stupid to give way to excesses of fear, but the authorities have thought it necessary to plaster the walls with cast, manifestly expensive, posters, headed with a Royal Crown, "Your courage, your resolution, your cheerfulness will bring us victory."

"Oh yus," said the London Cockney. "You'll get the victory all right. Trust you. On my courage, my resolution, my cheerfulness; you'll use up 'Tommy Atkins' all right. Larf at 'im in a kindly sort of way and use him. And then you think you'll out him back again on the dust-heap. Again? Twice?"

That is all too credible. But this time our rulers will emerge discredited and frustrated from the conflict to face a disorganised population in a state of mutinous enquiry. They have made preposterous promises to restore Poland and they will certainly have to eat their words about that. Or what is more probable the government will have to give place to another administration which will be able to eat those words for them with a slightly better grace. There is little prospect of Thanksgiving Services or any Armistice night orgy this time. People at home are tasting the hardships of war even more tediously and irritating than the men on active service. Cinemas, theatres, have been shut prematurely, black-outs have diminished the safety of the streets and doubled the tale of road casualties. The British crowd is already a sullen crowd. The world has not seen it in such a bad temper for a century and half, and, let there be no mistake about it, it is far less in a temper with the Germans than it is with its own rulers.

Through all this swirling intimidating propaganda of civil disorder and a systematic suppression of news and criticism of the most exasperating sort, war preparation has proceeded. The perplexed and baffled citizen can only hope that on the military side there has been a little more foresight and less hysteria.

The loss of confidence and particularly confidence in the government and social order is already enormous. No one feels secure, in his job, in his services, in his savings, any longer. People lose confidence even in the money in their pockets. And human society is built on confidence. It cannot carry on without it.

Things are like this already and it is only the opening stage of this strange war. The position of the ruling class and the financial people who have hitherto dominated British affairs is a peculiar one. The cast of the war is already enormous, and there is no sign that it will diminish. Income tax, super tax, death duties, taxes on war profits have been raised to a level that should practically extinguish the once prosperous middle strata of society altogether. The very wealthy will survive in a shorn and diminished state, they will hang on to the last, but the graded classes that have hitherto intervened between them and the impoverished masses of the population, who will be irritated by war sacrifices, extensively unemployed and asking more and more penetrating questions, will have diminished greatly. Only by the most ingenious monetary manipulation, by dangerous tax-dodging and expedients verging on sheer scoundrelism, will a clever young man have the ghost of a chance of climbing by the old traditional money-making ladder, above his fellows. On the other hand, the career of a public employee will become continually more attractive. There is more interest in it and more self-respect. The longer the war continues, the completer and more plainly irreparable will be the dissolution of the old order.

Now to many readers who have been incredulous of the statement of the first section of this book, that we are living in the End of an Age, to those who have been impervious to the account of the disruptive forces that are breaking up the social order and to the argument I have drawn from them, who may have got away from all that, so to speak, by saying they are "scientific" or "materialistic" or "sociological" or "highbrow", or that Providence that has hitherto displayed such a marked bias in favour of well-off, comfortable, sluggish-minded people is sure to do something nice for them at the eleventh hour, the real inconveniences, alarms, losses and growing disorder of the life about them may at last bring a realisation that the situation in Western Europe is approaching revolutionary conditions. It will be a hard saying for many people in the advantage-holding classes, and particularly if they are middle-aged, that the older has already gone to pieces can never be put back. But how can they doubt it?

A revolution, that is to say a more or less convulsive effort at social and political readjustment, is bound to come in all these overstrained countries, in Germany, in Britain and universally. It is more likely than not to arise directly out of the exasperating diminuendos and crescendos of the present war, as a culminating phase of it. Revolution of some sort we must have. We cannot prevent its onset. But we can affect the course of its development. It may end in utter disaster or it may release a new world, far better than the old. Within these broad limits it is possible for us to make up our minds how it will come to us.

And since the only practical question before us is the question of how we will take this world revolution we cannot possibly evade, let me recall to your attention the reasons I have advanced in the second section of this book for the utmost public discussion of our situation at the present time. And also let me bring back to mind the examination of Marxism in the fourth section. There it is shown how easily a collectivist movement, especially when it is faced by the forcible-feeble resistances and suppressions of those who have hitherto enjoyed wealth and power, may degenerate into an old-fashioned class-war, become conspiratorial, dogmatic and inadaptable, and sink towards leader worship and autocracy. That apparently is what has happened in Russia in its present phase. We do not know how much of the original revolutionary spirit survives there, and a real fundamental issue in the world situation is whether we are to follow in the footsteps of Russia or whether we are going to pull ourselves together, face the stern logic of necessity and produce a Western Revolution, which will benefit by the Russian experience, react upon Russia and lead ultimately to a world understanding.

What is it that the Atlantic world finds most objectionable in the Soviet world of to-day? Is it any disapproval of collectivism as such? Only in the case of a dwindling minority of rich and successful men - and very rarely of the sons of such people. Very few capable men under fifty nowadays remain individualists in political and social matters. They are not even fundamentally anti-Communist. Only it happens that for various reasons the political life of the community is still in the hands of unteachable old-fashioned people. What are called "democracies" suffer greatly from the rule of old men who have not kept pace with the times. The real and effective disapproval, distrust and disbelief in the soundness of the Soviet system lies not in the out-of-date individualism of these elderly types, but in the conviction that it can never achieve

59

efficiency or even maintain its honest ideal of each for all and all for each, unless it has free speech and an insistence upon legally-defined freedoms for the individual within the collectivist framework. We do not deplore the Russian Revolution as a Revolution. We complain that it is not a good enough Revolution and we want a better one.

The more highly things are collectivised the more necessary is a legal system embodying the Rights of Man. This has been forgotten under the Soviets, and so men go in fear there of arbitrary police action. But the more functions your government controls the more need there is for protective law. The objection to Soviet collectivism is that, lacking the antiseptic of legally assured personal freedom, it will not keep. It professes to be fundamentally a common economic system based on class-war ideas; the industrial director is under the heel of the Party commissar; the political police have got altogether out of hand; and the affairs gravitate inevitably towards an oligarchy or an autocracy protecting its incapacity by the repression of adverse comment.

But these valid criticisms merely indicate the sort of collectivisation that has to be avoided. It does not dispose of collectivism as such. If we in our turn do not wish to be submerged by the wave of Bolshevisation that is evidently advancing from the East, we must implement all these valid objections and create a collectivisation that will be more efficient, more prosperous, tolerant, free and rapidly progressive than the system we condemn. We, who do not like the Stalinised-Marxist state, have, as they used to say in British politics, to "dish" it by going one better. We have to confront Eastern-spirited collectivism with Western-spirited collectivism.

Perhaps this may be better put. We may be giving way to a sub-conscious conceit here and assuming that the West is always going to be thinking more freely and clearly and working more efficiently than the East. It is like that now, but it may not always be like that. Every country has had its phases of illumination and its phases of blindness. Stalin and Stalinism are neither the beginning nor the end of the collectivisation of Russia.

We are dealing with something still almost impossible to estimate, the extent to which the new Russian patriotism and the new Stalin-worship, have effaced and how far they have merely masked, the genuinely creative international communism of the revolutionary years. The Russian mind is not a docile mind, and most of the literature available for a young man to read in Russia, we must remember, is still revolutionary. There has been no burning of the books there. The Moscow radio talks for internal consumption since the Hitler-Stalin understanding betray a great solicitude on the part of the government to make it clear that there has been no sacrifice of revolutionary principle. That witnesses to the vitality of public opinion in Russia. The clash between the teachings of 1920 and 1940 may have a liberating effect on many people's minds. Russians love to talk about ideas. Under the Czar they talked. It is incredible that they do not talk under Stalin.

That question whether collectivisation is to be "Westernised" or "Easternised", using these words under the caveat of the previous paragraph, is really the first issue before the world to-day. We need a fully ventilated Revolution. Our Revolution has to go on in the light and air. We may have to accept sovietisation à la Russe quite soon unless we can produce a better collectivisation. But if we produce a better collectivisation it is more probable than not that the Russian system will incorporate our improvements, forget its reviving nationalism again, debunk Marx and Stalin, so far as they can be debunked, and merge into the one world state.

Between these primary antagonists, between Revolution with its eyes open and Revolution with a mask and a gag, there will certainly be complications of the issue due to patriotism and bigotry and the unteachable wilful blindness of those who do not want to see. Most people lie a lot to themselves before they lie to other people, and it is hopeless to expect that all the warring cults and traditions that confuse the mind of the race to-day are going to fuse under a realisation of the imperative nature of the human situation as I have stated it here. Multitudes will never realise it. Few human+beings are able to change their primary ideas after the middle thirties. They get fixed in them and drive before them no more intelligently than animals drive before their innate impulses. They will die rather than change their second selves.

One of the most entangling of these disconcerting secondary issues is that created by the stupid and persistent intrigues of the Roman Catholic Church.

Let me be clear here. I am speaking of the Vatican and of its sustained attempts to exercise a directive rôle in secular life. I number among my friends many Roman Catholics who have built the most charming personalities and behaviour systems on the framework provided them by their faith. One of the loveliest characters I have ever known was G. K. Chesterton. But I think he was just as fine before he became a Catholic as afterwards. Still he found something he needed in Catholicism. There are saints of all creeds and of none, so good are better possibilities of human nature. Religious observances provide a frame that many find indispensable for the seemly ordering of their lives. And outside the ranks of "strict" observers many good people with hardly more theology than a Unitarian, love to speak of goodness and kindness as Christianity. So-and-so is a "good Christian". Voltaire, says Alfred Noyes, the Catholic writer, was a "good Christian". I do not use the word "Christianity" in that sense because I do not believe that Christians have any monopoly of goodness. When I write of Christianity, I mean Christianity with a definite creed and militant organisation and not these good kind people, good and kind but not very fastidious about the exact use of the words.

Such "good Christians" can be almost as bitterly critical as I am of the continual pressure upon the faithful by that inner group of Italians in Rome, subsidised by the Fascist government, who pull the strings of Church policy throughout the world, so as to do this or that tortuous or uncivilised thing, to cripple education, to persecute unorthodox ways of living.

It is to the influence of the Church that we must ascribe the foolish support by the British Foreign Office of Franco, that murderous little "Christian gentleman", in his overthrow of the staggering liberal renascence of Spain. It is the Roman Catholic influence the British and French have to thank, for the fantastic blundering that involved them in the defence of the impossible Polish state and its unrighteous acquisitions; it affected British policy in respect to Austria and Czechoslovakia profoundly, and now it is doing its utmost to maintain and develop a political estrangement between Russia and the Western world by its prejudiced exacerbation of the idea that Russia is "anti-

God" while we Westerners are little children of the light, gallantly fighting on the side of the Cross, Omnipotence, Greater Poland, national sovereignty, the small uneconomic prolific farmer and shopkeeper and anything else you like to imagine constitutes "Christendom".

The Vatican strives perpetually to develop the present war into a religious war. It is trying to steal the war. By all the circumstances of its training it is unteachable. It knows no better. It will go on - until some economic revolution robs it of its funds. Then as a political influence it may evaporate very rapidly. The Anglican Church and many other Protestant sects, the wealthy Baptists, for example, follow suit.

It is not only in British affairs that this propaganda goes on. With the onset of war France becomes militant and Catholic. It has suppressed the Communist Party, as a gesture of resentment against Russia and a precaution against post-war collectivisation. The Belgian caricaturist Raemaekers is now presenting Hitler day after day as a pitiful weakling already disposed of and worthy of our sympathy, while Stalin is represented as a frightful giant with horns and a tail. Yet both France and Britain are at peace with Russia and have every reason to come to a working understanding with that country. The attitude of Russia to the war has on the whole been cold, contemptuous and reasonable.

It is not as if these devious schemes can take us somewhere; it is not that this restoration of the Holy Roman Empire is a possibility. You confront these Catholic politicians, just as you confront the politicians of Westminster, with these two cardinal facts, the abolition of distance and the change of scale. In vain. You cannot get any realisation of the significance of these things into those idea-proofed skulls. They are deaf to it, blind to it. They cannot see that it makes any difference at all to their long-established mental habits. If their minds waver for a moment they utter little magic prayers to exorcise the gleam.

What, they ask, has "mere size" to do with the soul of man, "mere speed, mere power"? What can the young do better than subdue their natural urgency to live and do? What has mere life to do with the religious outlook? The war, these Vatican propagandists insist, is a "crusade" against modernism, against socialism and free thought, the restoration of priestly authority is its end; our sons are fighting to enable the priest to thrust his pious uncleanliness once again between reader and book, child and knowledge, husband and wife, sons and lovers. While honest men are fighting now to put an end to military aggression, to resume indeed that "war to end war" that was aborted to give us the League of Nations, these bigots are sedulously perverting the issue, trying to represent it as a religious war against Russia in particular and the modern spirit in general.

The well-trained Moslem, the American fundamentalists, the orthodox Jew, all the fixed cultures, produce similar irrelevant and wasteful resistances, but the Catholic organisation reaches further and is more persistent. It is frankly opposed to human effort and the idea of progress. It makes no pretence about it.

Such cross-activities as these complicate, delay and may even sabotage effectively every effort to solve the problem of a lucid collectivisation of the world's affairs, but they do not alter the essential fact that it is only through a rationalisation and coalescence of constructive revolutionary movements everywhere and a liberal triumph over the dogmatism of the class war, that we can hope to emerge from the present wreckage of our world.

Chapter 7

Federation

Let us now take up certain vaguely constructive proposals which seem at present to be very much in people's minds. They find their cardinal expression in a book called Union Now by Mr Clarence K. Streit, which has launched the magic word "Federation" upon the world. The "democracies" of the world are to get together upon a sort of enlargement of the Federal constitution of the United States (which produced one of the bloodiest civil wars in all history) and then all will be well with us.

Let us consider whether this word "Federation" is of any value in organising the Western Revolution. I would suggest it is. I think it may be a means of mental release for many people who would otherwise have remained dully resistant to any sort of change.

This Federation project has an air of reasonableness. It is attractive to a number of influential people who wish with the minimum of adaptation to remain influential in a changing world, and particularly is it attractive to what I may call the liberal-conservative elements of the prosperous classes in America and Great Britain and the Oslo countries, because it puts the most difficult aspect of the problem, the need for collective socialisation, so completely in the background that it can be ignored. This enables them to take quite a bright and hopeful view of the future without any serious hindrance to their present preoccupations.

They think that Federation, reasonably defined, may suspend the possibility of war for a considerable period and so lighten the burden of taxation that the present crushing demands on them will relax and they will be able to resume, on a slightly more economical scale perhaps, their former way of living. Everything that gives them hope and self-respect and preserves their homes from the worst indignities of panic, appeasement, treason-hunting and the rest of it, is to be encouraged, and meanwhile their sons will have time to think and it may be possible so to search, ransack and rationalise the Streit project as to make a genuine and workable scheme for the socialisation of the world.

In The Fate of Homo sapiens I examined the word "democracy" with some care, since it already seemed likely that great quantities of our young men were to be asked to cripple and risk their lives for its sake. I showed that it was still a very incompletely realised aspiration, that its complete development involved socialism and a level of education and information attained as yet by no community in the world. Mr Streit gives a looser, more rhetorical statement - a more idealistic statement, shall we say? - of his conception of democracy, the sort of statement that would be considered wildly exaggerated even if it was war propaganda, and though unhappily it is remote from any achieved reality, he proceeds without further enquiry as if it were a description of existing realities in what he calls the "democracies" of the world. In them he imagines he finds "governments of the people, by the people, for the people".

In the book I have already cited I discuss What is Democracy?
And Where is Democracy? I do my best there to bring Mr
Streit down to the harsh and difficult facts of the case. I will go
now a little more into particulars in my examination of his
project.

His "founder democracies" are to be: "The American Union,
the British Commonwealth (specifically the United Kingdom,
the Federal Dominion of Canada, the Commonwealth of
Australia, New Zealand, the Union of South Africa, Ireland),
the French Republic, Belgium, the Netherlands, the Swiss
Confederation, Denmark, Norway, Sweden and Finland."

Scarcely one of these, as I have shown in that former book, is
really a fully working democracy. And the Union of South
Africa is a particularly bad and dangerous case of race tyranny.
Ireland is an incipient religious war and not one country but
two. Poland, I note, does not come into Mr Streit's list of
democracies at all. His book was written in 1938 when Poland
was a totalitarian country holding, in defiance of the League of
Nations, Vilna, which it had taken from Lithuania, large areas
of non-Polish country it had conquered from Russia, and
fragments gained by the dismemberment of Czechoslovakia. It
only became a democracy, even technically and for a brief
period, before its collapse in September 1939, when Mr
Chamberlain was so foolish as to drag the British Empire into a
costly and perilous war, on its behalf. But that is by the way.
None of these fifteen (or ten) "founder democracies" are really
democracies at all. So we start badly. But they might be made
socialist democracies and their federation might be made
something very real indeed - at a price. The U.S.S.R. is a
federated socialist system, which has shown a fairly successful

69

political solidarity during the past two decades, whatever else it has done or failed to do.

Now let us help Mr Streit to convert his "federation" from a noble but extremely rhetorical aspiration into a living reality. He is aware that this must be done at a price, but I want to suggest that that price is, from what I judge to be his point of view, far greater, and the change much simpler, more general and possibly even closer at hand, than he supposes. He is disposed to appeal to existing administrative organisations, and it is questionable whether they are the right people to execute his designs. One of the difficulties he glosses over is the possible reluctance of the India Office to hand over the control of India (Ceylon and Burma he does not mention) to the new Federation Government, which would also, I presume, take charge of the fairly well governed and happy fifty-odd million people of the Dutch East Indies, the French colonial empire, the West Indies and so on. This, unless he proposes merely to re-christen the India Office, etc., is asking for an immense outbreak of honesty and competence on the part of the new Federal officialdom. It is also treating the possible contribution of these five or six hundred million of dusky peoples to the new order with a levity inconsistent with democratic ideals.

Quite a lot of these people have brains which are as good or better than normal European brains. You could educate the whole world to the not very exalted level of a Cambridge graduate in a single lifetime, if you had schools, colleges, apparatus and teachers enough. The radio, the cinema, the gramophone, the improvements in both production and distribution, have made it possible to increase the range and effectiveness of a gifted teacher a thousandfold. We have seen intensive war preparations galore, but no one has dreamt yet of an intensive educational effort. None of us really like to see other people being educated. They may be getting an advantage over our privileged selves. Suppose we overcome that primitive jealousy. Suppose we speed up - as we are now physically able to do - the education and enfranchisement of these huge undeveloped reservoirs of human capacity. Suppose we tack that on the Union Now idea. Suppose we stipulate that Federation, wherever it extends, means a New and Powerful Education. In Bengal, in Java, in the Congo Free State, quite as much as in Tennessee or Georgia or Scotland or Ireland. Suppose we think a little less about "gradual enfranchisement" by votes and experiments in local autonomy and all these old ideas, and a little more about the enfranchisement of the mind. Suppose we drop that old cant about politically immature peoples.

There is one direction in which Mr Streit's proposals are open to improvement. Let us turn to another in which he does not seem to have realised all the implications of his proposal. This great Union is to have a union money and a union customs-free economy. What follows upon that? More I think than he realises.

There is one aspect of money to which the majority of those that discuss it seem to be incurably blind. You cannot have a theory of money or any plan about money by itself in the air. Money is not a thing in itself; it is a working part of an economic system. Money varies in its nature with the laws and ideas of property in a community. As a community moves towards collectivism and communism, for example, money simplifies out. Money is a necessary in a communism as it is in any other system, but its function therein is at its simplest. Payment in kind to the worker gives him no freedom of choice

71

among the goods the community produces. Money does. Money becomes the incentive that "works the worker" and nothing more.

But directly you allow individuals not only to obtain goods for consumption, but also to obtain credit to produce material for types of production outside the staple productions of the state, the question of credit and debt arises and money becomes more complicated. With every liberation of this or that product or service from collective control to business or experimental exploitation, the play of the money system enlarges and the laws regulating what you may take for it, the company laws, bankruptcy laws and so forth increase. In any highly developed collective system the administration will certainly have to give credits for hopeful experimental enterprises. When the system is not collectivism, monetary operations for gain are bound to creep in and become more and more complicated. Where most of the substantial side of life is entrusted to uncoordinated private enterprise, the intricacy of the money apparatus increases enormously. Monetary manipulation becomes a greater and greater factor in the competitive struggle, not only between individuals and firms, but between states. As Mr Streit himself shows, in an excellent discussion of the abandonment of the gold standard, inflation and deflation become devices in international competition. Money becomes strategic, just as pipe lines and railways can become strategic.

This being so it is plain that for the Federal Union a common money means an identical economic life throughout the Union. And this too is implied also in Mr Streit's "customs-free" economy. It is impossible to have a common money when a dollar or a pound, or whatever it is, can buy this, that or the other advantage in one state and is debarred from anything but bare purchases for consumption in another. So that this Federal Union is bound to be a uniform economic system. There can be only very slight variations in the control of economic life.

In the preceding sections the implacable forces that make for the collectivisation of the world or disaster, have been exposed. It follows that "Federation" means practically uniform socialism within the Federal limits, leading, as state after state is incorporated, to world socialism. There manifestly we carry Mr Streit farther than he realises he goes - as yet. For it is fairly evident that he is under the impression that a large measure of independent private business is to go on throughout the Union. I doubt if he imagines it is necessary to go beyond the partial socialisation already achieved by the New Deal. But we have assembled evidence to show that the profit scramble, the wild days of uncorrelated "business" are over for ever.

And again though he realises and states very clearly that governments are made for man and not man for governments, though he applauds the great declarations of the Convention that created the American Constitution, wherein "we the people of the United States" overrode the haggling of the separate states and established the American Federal Constitution, nevertheless he is curiously chary of superseding any existing legal governments in the present world. He is chary of talking of "We the people of the world". But many of us are coming to realise that all existing governments have to go into the melting pot, we believe that it is a world revolution which is upon us, and that in the great struggle to evoke a Westernised World Socialism, contemporary governments may vanish like straw hats in the rapids of Niagara. Mr Streit, however, becomes extraordinarily legal-minded at this stage. I do not think that he realises the forces of destruction that are gathering and so I

think he hesitates to plan a reconstruction upon anything like
the scale that may become possible.

He evades even the obvious necessity that under a Federal
Government the monarchies of Great Britain, Belgium,
Norway, Sweden, Holland, if they survive at all, must becomes
like the mediatised sovereigns of the component states of the
former German Empire, mere ceremonial vestiges. Perhaps he
thinks that, but he does not say it outright. I do not know if he
has pondered the New York World Fair of 1939 nor the
significance of the Royal Visit to America in that year, and
thought how much there is in the British system that would
have to be abandoned if his Federation is to become a reality.
In most of the implications of the word, it must cease to be
"British". His Illustrative Constitution is achieved with an
altogether forensic disregard of the fundamental changes in
human conditions to which we have to adapt ourselves or
perish. He thinks of war by itself and not as an eruption due to
deeper maladaptations. But if we push his earlier stipulations to
their necessary completion, we need not trouble very much
about that sample constitution of his, which is to adjust the
balance so fairly among the constituent states. The abolition of
distance must inevitably substitute functional associations and
loyalties for local attributions, if human society does not break
up altogether. The local divisions will melt into a world
collectivity and the main conflicts in a progressively unifying
Federation are much more likely to be these between different
world-wide types and associations of workers.

So far with Union Now. One of Mr Streit's outstanding merits
is that he has had the courage to make definite proposals on
which we can bite. I doubt if a European could have produced
any such book. Its naïve political legalism, its idea of salvation

by constitution, and its manifest faith in the magic beneficence of private enterprise, are distinctly in the vein of an American, almost a pre-New Deal American, who has become, if anything, more American, through his experiences of the deepening disorder of Europe. So many Americans still look on at world affairs like spectators at a ball game who are capable of vociferous participation but still have no real sense of participation; they do not realise that the ground is moving under their seats also, and that the social revolution is breaking surface to engulf them in their turn. To most of us - to most of us over forty at any rate - the idea of a fundamental change in our way of life is so unpalatable that we resist it to the last moment.

Mr Streit betrays at times as vivid a sense of advancing social collapse as I have, but it has still to occur to him that that collapse may be conclusive. There may be dark ages, a relapse into barbarism, but somewhen and somehow he thinks man must recover. George Bernard Shaw has recently been saying the same thing.

It may be worse that that.

I have given Mr Streit scarcely a word of praise, because that would be beside the mark here. He wrote his book sincerely as a genuine contribution to the unsystematic world conference that is now going on, admitting the possibility of error, demanding criticism, and I have dealt with it in that spirit.

Unfortunately his word has gone much further than his book. His book says definite things and even when one disagrees with it, it is good as a point of departure. But a number of people have caught up this word "Federation", and our minds are distracted by a multitude of appeals to support Federal projects with the most various content or with no content at all.

All the scores and hundreds of thousands of nice people who are signing peace pledges and so forth a few years ago, without the slightest attempt in the world to understand what they meant by peace, are now echoing this new magic word with as little conception of any content for it. They did not realise that peace means so complicated and difficult an ordering and balancing of human society that it has never been sustained since man became man, and that we have wars and preparatory interludes between wars because that is a much simpler and easier sequence for our wilful, muddle-headed, suspicious and aggressive species. These people still think we can get this new and wonderful state of affairs just by clamouring for it.

And having failed to get peace by saying "Peace" over and over again, they are now with an immense sense of discovery saying "Federation". What must happen to men in conspicuous public positions I do not know, but even an irresponsible literary man like myself finds himself inundated with innumerable lengthy private letters, hysterical post-cards, pamphlets from budding organisations, "declarations" to sign, demands for subscriptions, all in the name of the new panacea, all as vain and unproductive as the bleating of lost sheep. And I cannot open a newspaper without finding some eminent contemporary writing a letter to it, saying gently, firmly and bravely, the same word, sometimes with bits of Union Now tacked on to it, and sometimes with minor improvements, but often with nothing more than the bare idea.

All sorts of idealistic movements for world peace which have been talking quietly to themselves for years and years have been stirred up to follow the new banner. Long before the Great War there was a book by Sir Max Waechter, a friend of King Edward the Seventh, advocating the United States of Europe, and that inexact but flattering parallelism to the United States of America has recurred frequently; as a phase thrown out by Monsieur Briand for example, and as a project put forward by an Austrian-Japanese writer, Count Coudenhove-Kalergi, who even devised a flag for the Union. The main objection to the idea is that there are hardly any states completely in Europe, except Switzerland, San Marino, Andorra and a few of the Versailles creations. Almost all the other European states extend far beyond the European limits both politically and in their sympathies and cultural relations. They trail with them more than half mankind. About a tenth of the British Empire is in Europe and still less of the Dutch Empire; Russia, Turkey, France, are less European than not; Spain and Portugal have their closest links with South America.

Few Europeans think of themselves as "Europeans". I, for example, am English, and a large part of my interests, intellectual and material, are Transatlantic. I dislike calling myself "British" and I like to think of myself as a member of a great English-speaking community, which spreads irrespective of race and colour round and about the world. I am annoyed when an American calls me a "foreigner" - war with America would seem to me just as insane as war with Cornwall - and I find the idea of cutting myself off from the English-speaking peoples of America and Asia to follow the flag of my Austrian-Japanese friend into a federally bunched-up European extremely unattractive.

It would, I suggest, be far easier to create the United States of the World, which is Mr Streit's ultimate objective, than to get together the so-called continent of Europe into any sort of unity.

I find most of these United States of Europe movements are now jumping on to the Federation band-wagon.

My old friend and antagonist, Lord David Davies, for instance, has recently succumbed to the infection. He was concerned about the problem of a World Pax in the days when the League of Nations Society and other associated bodies were amalgamated in the League of Nations Union. He was struck then by an idea, an analogy, and the experience was unique for him. He asked why individuals went about in modern communities in nearly perfect security from assault and robbery, without any need to bear arms. His answer was the policeman. And from that he went on to the question of what was needed for states and nations to go their ways with the same blissful immunity from violence and plunder, and it seemed to him a complete and reasonable answer to say "an international policeman". And there you were! He did not see, he is probably quite incapable of seeing, that a state is something quite different in its nature and behaviour from an individual human+being. When he was asked to explain how that international policeman was to be created and sustained, he just went on saying "international policeman". He has been saying it for years. Sometimes it seems it is to be the League of Nations, sometimes the British Empire, sometimes an international Air Force, which is to undertake this grave responsibility. The bench before which the policeman is to hale the offender and this position of the lock-up are not indicated. Finding our criticisms uncongenial, his lordship went off with his great idea, like a penguin which has found an egg, to incubate it alone. I hope he will be spared to say "international policeman" for many years to come, but I do not believe he has ever perceived or ever will perceive that, brilliant as his inspiration was, it still left vast areas of the problem in darkness. Being a man of considerable means, he has been able to sustain a "New Commonwealth" movement and publish books and a periodical in which his one great idea is elaborated rather than developed.

But I will not deal further with the very incoherent multitude that now echoes this word "Federation". Many among them will cease to cerebrate further and fall by the wayside, but many will go on thinking, and if they go on thinking they will come to perceive more and more clearly the realities of the case. Federation, they will feel, is not enough.

So much for the present "Federalist" front. As a fundamental basis of action, as a declared end, it seems hopelessly vague and confused and, if one may coin a phrase, hopelessly optimistic. But since the concept seems to be the way to release a number of minds from belief in the sufficiency of a League of Nations, associated or not associated with British Imperialism, it has been worth while to consider how it can be amplified and turned in the direction of that full and open-eyed world-wide collectivisation which a study of existing conditions obliges us to believe is the only alternative to the complete degeneration of our species.

H. G. Wells

Chapter 8

The New Type of Revolution

Let us return to our main purpose, which is to examine the way in which we are to face up to this impending World Revolution.

To many minds this idea of Revolution is almost inseparable from visions of street barricades made of paving-stones and overturned vehicles, ragged mobs armed with impromptu weapons and inspired by defiant songs, prisons broken and a general jail delivery, palaces stormed, a great hunting of ladies and gentlemen, decapitated but still beautiful heads on pikes, regicides of the most sinister quality, the busy guillotine, a crescendo of disorder ending in a whiff of grapeshot. . . .

That was one type of Revolution. It is what one might call the Catholic type of Revolution, that it is to say it is the ultimate phase of a long period of Catholic living and teaching. People do not realise this and some will be indignant at its being stated so barely. Yet the facts stare us in the face, common knowledge, not to be denied. That furious, hungry, desperate, brutal mob was the outcome of generations of Catholic rule, Catholic morality and Catholic education. The King of France was the "Most Christian King, the eldest son of the Church", he was master of the economic and financial life of the community, and the Catholic Church controlled the intellectual

81

life of the community and the education of the people absolutely. That mob was the outcome. It is absurd to parrot that Christianity has never been tried. Christianity in its most highly developed form has been tried and tried again. It was tried for centuries fully and completely, in Spain, France, Italy. It was responsible for the filth and chronic pestilence and famine of medieval England. It inculcated purity but it never inculcated cleanliness. Catholic Christianity had practically unchallenged power in France for generations. It was free to teach as it chose and as much as it chose. It dominated the common life entirely. The Catholic system in France cannot have reaped anything it did not sow, for no other sowers were allowed. That hideous mob of murderous ragamuffins we are so familiar with in pictures of the period, was the final harvest of its regime.

The more Catholic reactionaries revile the insurgent common people of the first French Revolution, the more they condemn themselves. It is the most impudent perversion of reality for them to snivel about the guillotine and the tumbrils, as though these were not purely Catholic products, as though they came in suddenly from outside to wreck a genteel Paradise. They were the last stage of the systematic injustice and ignorance of a strictly Catholic regime. One phase succeeded another with relentless logic. The Maseillaise completed the life-cycle of Catholicism.

In Spain too and in Mexico we have seen undisputed educational and moral Catholic ascendancy, the Church with a free hand, producing a similar uprush of blind resentment. The crowds there also were cruel and blasphemous; but Catholicism cannot complain; for Catholicism hatched them. Priests and nuns who had been the sole teachers of the people were insulted and outraged and churches defiled. Surely if the Church is anything like what it claims to be, the people would have loved it. They would not have behaved as though sacrilege was a gratifying relief.

But these Catholic Revolutions are only specimens of one single type of Revolution. A Revolution need not be a spontaneous storm of indignation against intolerable indignities and deprivations. It can take quite other forms.

As a second variety of Revolution, which is in sharp contrast with the indignation-revolt in which so many periods of unchallenged Catholic ascendancy have ended, we may take what we may call the "revolution conspiracy", in which a number of people set about organising the forces of discomfort and resentment and loosening the grip of the government's forces, in order to bring about a fundamental change of system. The ideal of this type is the Bolshevik Revolution in Russia, provided it is a little simplified and misunderstood. This, reduced to a working theory by its advocates, is conceived of as a systematic cultivation of a public state of mind favourable to a Revolution together with an inner circle of preparation for a "seizure of power". Quite a number of Communist and other leftish writers, bright young men, without much political experience, have let their imaginations loose upon the "technique" of such an adventure. They have brought the Nazi and Fascist Revolutions into the material for their studies. Modern social structure with its concentration of directive, information and coercive power about radio stations, telephone exchangers, newspaper offices, police stations, arsenals and the like, lends itself to quasi-gangster exploitation of this type. There is a great rushing about and occupation of key centres, an organised capture, imprisonment or murder of possible

83

opponents, and the country is confronted with fait accompli. The regimentation of the more or less reluctant population follows.

But a Revolution need be neither an explosion nor a coup d'état. And the Revolution that lies before us now as the only hopeful alternative to chaos, either directly or after an interlude of world communism, is to be attained, if it is attained at all, by neither of these methods. The first is too rhetorical and chaotic and leads simply to a Champion and tyranny; the second is too conspiratorial and leads through an obscure struggle of masterful personalities to a similar end. Neither is lucid enough and deliberate enough to achieve a permanent change in the form and texture of human affairs.

An altogether different type of Revolution may or may not be possible. No one can say that it is possible unless it is tried, but one can say with some assurance that unless it can be achieved the outlook for mankind for many generations at least is hopeless. The new Revolution aims essentially at a change in directive ideas. In its completeness it is an untried method.

It depends for its success upon whether a sufficient number of minds can be brought to realise that the choice before us now is not a choice between further revolution or more or less reactionary conservatism, but a choice between so carrying on and so organising the process of change in our affairs as to produce a new world order, or suffering an entire and perhaps irreparable social collapse. Our argument throughout has been that things have gone too far ever to be put back again to any similitude of what they have been. We can no more dream of remaining where we are than think of going back in the middle of a dive. We must go trough with these present changes, adapt

84

ourselves to them, adjust ourselves to the plunge, or be destroyed by them. We must go through these changes just as we must go through this ill-conceived war, because there is as yet no possible end for it.

There will be no possible way of ending it until the new Revolution defines itself. If it is patched up now without a clear-headed settlement understood and accepted throughout the world, we shall have only the simulacrum of a peace. A patched-up peace now will not even save us from the horrors of war, it will postpone them only to aggravate them in a few years time. You cannot end this war yet, you can at best adjourn it.

The reorganisation of the world has at first to be mainly the work of a "movement" or a Party or a religion or cult, whatever we choose to call it. We may call it New Liberalism or the New Radicalism or what not. It will not be a close-knit organisation, toeing the Party line and so forth. It may be a very loose-knit and many faceted, but if a sufficient number of minds throughout the world, irrespective of race, origin or economic and social habituations, can be brought to the free and candid recognition of the essentials of the human problem, then their effective collaboration in a conscious, explicit and open effort to reconstruct human society will ensue.

And to begin with they will do all they can to spread and perfect this conception of a new world order, which they will regard as the only working frame for their activities, while at the same time they will set themselves to discover and associate with themselves, everyone, everywhere, who is intellectually able to grasp the same broad ideas and morally disposed to realise them.

85

H. G. Wells

The distribution of this essential conception one may call propaganda, but in reality it is education. The opening phase of this new type of Revolution must involve therefore a campaign for re-invigorated and modernised education throughout the world, an education that will have the same ratio to the education of a couple of hundred years ago, as the electric lighting of a contemporary city has to the chandeliers and oil lamps of the same period. On its present mental levels humanity can do no better than what it is doing now.

Vitalising education is only possible when it is under the influence of people who are themselves learning. It is inseparable from the modern idea of education that it should be knit up to incessant research. We say research rather than science. It is the better word because it is free from any suggestion of that finality which means dogmatism and death.

All education tends to become stylistic and sterile unless it is kept in close touch with experimental verification and practical work, and consequently this new movement of revolutionary initiative, must at the same time be sustaining realistic political and social activities and working steadily for the collectivisation of governments and economic life. The intellectual movement will be only the initiatory and correlating part of the new revolutionary drive. These practical activities must be various. Everyone engaged in them must be thinking for himself and not waiting for orders. The only dictatorship he will recognise is the dictatorship of the plain understanding and the invincible fact.

And if this culminating Revolution is to be accomplished, then the participation of every conceivable sort of human+being

86

who has the mental grasp to see these broad realities of the world situation and the moral quality to do something about it, must be welcomed.

Previous revolutionary thrusts have been vitiated by bad psychology. They have given great play to the gratification of the inferiority complexes that arise out of class disadvantages. It is no doubt very unjust that anyone should be better educated, healthier and less fearful of the world than anyone else, but that is no reason why the new Revolution should not make the fullest use of the health, education, vigour and courage of the fortunate. The Revolution we are contemplating will aim at abolishing the bitterness of frustration. But certainly it will do nothing to avenge it. Nothing whatever. Let the dead past punish its dead.

It is one of the most vicious streaks in the Marxist teaching to suggest that all people of wealth and capacity living in a community in which unco-ordinated private enterprise plays a large part are necessarily demoralised by the advantages they enjoy and that they must be dispossessed by the worker and peasant, who are presented as endowed with a collective virtue capable of running all the complex machinery of a modern community. But the staring truth of the matter is that an unco-ordinated scramble between individuals and nations alike, demoralises all concerned. Everyone is corrupted, the filching tramp by the roadside, the servile hand-kissing peasant of Eastern Europe, the dole-bribed loafer, as much as the woman who marries for money, the company promoter, the industrial organiser, the rent-exacting landlord and the diplomatic agent. When the social atmosphere is tainted everybody is ill.

Wealth, personal freedom and education, may and do produce wasters and oppressive people, but they may also release creative and administrative minds to opportunity. The history of science and invention before the nineteenth century confirms this. On the whole if we are to assume there is anything good in humanity at all, it is more reasonable to expect it to appear when there is most opportunity.

And in further confutation of the Marxist caricature of human motives, we have the very considerable number of young people drawn from middle-class and upper-class homes, who figure in the extreme left movement everywhere. It is their moral reaction to the "stuffiness" and social ineffectiveness of their parents and their own sort of people. They seek an outlet for their abilities that is not gainful but serviceable. Many have sought an honourable life - and often found it, and death with it - in the struggle against the Catholics and their Moorish and Fascist helpers in Spain.

It is a misfortune of their generation, that so many of them have fallen into the mental traps of Marxism. It has been my absurd experience to encounter noisy meetings of expensive young men at Oxford, not one of them stunted physically as I was by twenty years of under-nourishment and devitalised upbringing, all pretending to be rough-hewn collarless proletarians in shocked revolt against my bourgeois tyranny and the modest comfort of my declining years, and reciting the ridiculous class-war phrases by which they protected their minds from any recognition of the realities of the case. But though that attitude demonstrates the unstimulating education of their preparatory and public schools, which had thrown them thus uncritical and emotional into the problems of the undergraduate life, it does not detract from the fact that they had found the idea of abandoning themselves to a revolutionary reconstruction of society, that promised to end its enormous waste of potential happiness and achievement, extremely attractive, notwithstanding that their own advantages seemed to be reasonably secure.

Faced with the immediate approach of discomfort, indignity, wasted years, mutilation - death is soon over but one wakes up again to mutilation every morning - because of this ill-conceived war; faced also by the reversion of Russia to autocracy and the fiscal extinction of most of the social advantages of their families; these young people with a leftish twist are likely not only to do some very profitable re-examination of their own possibilities but also to find themselves joined in that re-examination by a very considerable number of others who have hitherto been repelled by the obvious foolishness and insincerity of the hammer and sickle symbols (workers and peasants of Oxford!) and the exasperating dogmatism of the orthodox Marxist. And may not these young people, instead of waiting to be overtaken by an insurrectionary revolution from which they will emerge greasy, unshaven, class-conscious and in incessant danger of liquidation, decide that before the Revolution gets hold of them they will get hold of the Revolution and save it from the inefficiency, mental distortions, disappointments and frustrations that have over-taken it in Russia.

This new and complete Revolution we contemplate can be defined in a very few words. It is (a) outright world-socialism, scientifically planned and directed, plus (b) a sustained insistence upon law, law based on a fuller, more jealously conceived resentment of the personal Rights of Man, plus (c) the completest freedom of speech, criticism and publication, and sedulous expansion of the educational organisation to the ever-growing demands of the new order. What we may call the eastern or Bolshevik Collectivism, the Revolution of the Internationale, has failed to achieve even the first of these three items and it has never even attempted the other two.

Putting it at its compactest, it is the triangle of Socialism, Law and Knowledge, which frames the Revolution which may yet save the world.

Socialism! Become outright collectivists? Very few men of the more fortunate classes in our old collapsing society who are over fifty will be able to readjust their minds to that. It will seem an entirely repulsive suggestion to them. (The average age of the British Cabinet at the present time is well over sixty.) But it need not be repulsive at all to their sons. They will be impoverished anyhow. The stars in their courses are seeing to that. And that will help them greatly to realise that an administrative control to administrative participation and then to direct administration are easy steps. They are being taken now, first in one matter and then in another. On both sides of the Atlantic. Reluctantly and often very disingenuously and against energetic but diminishing resistances. Great Britain, like America, may become a Socialist system with a definitive Revolution, protesting all the time that it is doing nothing of the sort.

In Britain we have now no distinctively educated class, but all up and down the social scale there are well-read men and women who have thought intensely upon these great problems we have been discussing. To many of them and maybe to enough of them to start the avalanche of purpose that will certainly develop from a clear and determined beginning, this conception of Revolution to evoke a liberal collectivised world may appeal. And so at last we narrow down our enquiry to an examination of what has to be done now to save the Revolution, what the movement or its Party - so far as it may use the semblance of a Party will do, what its Policy will be. Hitherto we have been demonstrating why a reasonable man, of any race or language anywhere, should become a "Western" Revolutionary. We have now to review the immediate activities to which he can give himself.

H. G. Wells

Chapter 9

Politics for the Sane Man

Let us restate the general conclusions to which our preceding
argument has brought us.

The establishment of a progressive world socialism in which
the freedoms, health and happiness of every individual are
protected by a universal law based on a re-declaration of the
rights of man, and wherein there is the utmost liberty of
thought, criticism and suggestion, is the plain, rational
objective before us now. Only the effective realisation of this
objective can establish peace on earth and arrest the present
march of human affairs to misery and destruction. We cannot
reiterate this objective too clearly and too frequently. The
triangle of collectivisation, law and knowledge should embody
the common purpose of all mankind.

But between us and that goal intervenes the vast and deepening
disorders of our time. The new order cannot be brought into
existence without a gigantic and more or less co-ordinated
effort of the saner and abler elements in the human population.
The thing cannot be done rapidly and melodramatically. That
effort must supply the frame for all sane social and political
activities and a practical criterion for all religious and
educational associations. But since our world is
multitudinously varied and confused, it is impossible to narrow

down this new revolutionary movement to any single class,
organisation or Party. It is too great a thing for that. It will in its
expansion produce and perhaps discard a number of
organisations and Parties, converging upon its ultimate
objective. Consequently, in order to review the social and
political activities of sane, clear-headed people to-day, we have
to deal with them piecemeal from a number of points of view.
We have to consider an advance upon a long and various front.

Let us begin then with the problem of sanity in face of the
political methods of our time. What are we to do as voting
citizens? There I think the history of the so-called democracies
in the past half-century is fairly conclusive. Our present
electoral methods which give no choice but a bilateral choice to
the citizen and so force a two-party system upon him, is a mere
caricature of representative government. It has produced upon
both sides of the Atlantic, big, stupid, and corrupt party
machines. That was bound to happen and yet to this day there
is a sort of shyness in the minds of young men interested in
politics when it comes to discussing Proportional
Representation. They think it is a "bit faddy". At best it is a
side issue. Party politicians strive to maintain that bashfulness,
because they know quite clearly that what is called
Proportional Representation with the single transferable vote in
large constituencies, returning a dozen members or more, is
extinction for the mere party hack and destruction for party
organisations.

The machine system in the United States is more elaborate,
more deeply entrenched legally in the Constitution and illegally
in the spoils system, and it may prove more difficult to
modernise than the British, which is based on an outworn caste
tradition. But both Parliament and Congress are essentially

similar in their fundamental quality. They trade in titles, concessions and the public welfare, and they are only amenable in the rough and at long last to the movements of public opinion. It is an open question whether they are much more responsive to popular feeling than the Dictators we denounce so unreservedly as the antithesis of democracy. They betray a great disregard of mass responses. They explain less. They disregard more. The Dictators have to go on talking and talking, not always truthfully but they have to talk. A dumb Dictator is inconceivable.

In such times of extensive stress and crisis as the present, the baffling slowness, inefficiency and wastefulness of the party system become so manifest that some of its worst pretences are put aside. The party game is suspended. His Majesty's Opposition abandons the pose of safeguarding the interests of the common citizens from those scoundrels upon the government benches; Republican and Democrats begin to cross the party line to discuss the new situation. Even the men who live professionally by the Parliamentary (Congressional) imposture, abandon it if they are sufficiently frightened by the posture of affairs. The appearance of an All-Party National Government in Great Britain before very long seems inevitable.

Great Britain has in effect gone socialist in a couple of months; she is also suspending party politics. Just as the United States did in the great slump. And in both cases this has happened because the rottenness and inefficiency of party politics stank to heaven in the face of danger. And since in both cases Party Government threw up its hands and bolted, is there any conceivable reason why we should let it come back at any appearance of victory or recovery, why we should not go ahead from where we are to a less impromptu socialist regime under a permanent non-party administration, to the reality if not to the form of a permanent socialist government?

Now here I have nothing to suggest about America. I have never, for example, tried to work out the consequences of the absence of executive ministers from the legislature. I am inclined to think that is one of the weak points in the Constitution and that the English usage which exposes the minister to question time in the House and makes him a prime mover in legislation affecting his department, is a less complicated and therefore more democratic arrangement than the American one. And the powers and functions of the President and the Senate are so different from the consolidated powers of Cabinet and Prime Minister, that even when an Englishman has industriously "mugged up" the constitutional points, he is still almost as much at a loss to get the living reality as he would be if he were shown the score of an opera before hearing it played or the blue prints of a machine he had never seen in action. Very few Europeans understand the history of Woodrow Wilson, the Senate and his League of Nations. They think that "America", which they imagine as a large single individual, planted the latter institution upon Europe and then deliberately shuffled out of her responsibility for it, and they will never think otherwise. And they think that "America" kept out of the war to the very limit of decency, overcharged us for munitions that contributed to the common victory, and made a grievance because the consequent debt was not discharged. They talk like that while Americans talk as if no English were killed between 1914 and 1918 (we had 800,000 dead) until the noble American conscripts came forward to die for them (to the tune of about 50,000). Savour for example even the title of Quincy Howe's England expects every American to do his Duty. It's the meanest of titles, but many Americans seem to like it.

On my desk as I write is a pamphlet by a Mr Robert Randall, nicely cyclostyled and got up. Which urges a common attack on the United States as a solution of the problem of Europe. No countries will ever feel united unless they have a common enemy, and the natural common enemy for Europe, it is declared, is the United States. So to bring about the United States of Europe we are to begin by denouncing the Monroe doctrine. I believe in the honesty and good intentions of Mr Robert Randall; he is, I am sure, no more in the pay of Germany, direct or indirect, than Mr Quincy Howe or Mr Harry Elmer Barnes; but could the most brilliant of Nazi war propagandists devise a more effective estranging suggestion? . .
.

But I wander from my topic. I do not know how sane men in America are going to set about relaxing the stranglehold of the Constitution, get control of their own country out of the hands of those lumpish, solemnly cunning politicians with their great strong jowls developed by chewing-gum and orotund speaking, whose photographs add a real element of frightfulness to the pages of Time, how they are going to abolish the spoils system, discover, and educate to expand a competent civil service able to redeem the hampered promises of the New Deal and pull America into line with the reconstruction of the rest of the world. But I perceive that in politics and indeed in most things, the underlying humour and sanity of Americans are apt to find a way round and do the impossible, and I have as little doubt they will manage it somehow as I have when I see a street performer on his little chair and carpet, all tied up with chains,

97

waiting until there are sufficient pennies in the hat to justify exertion.

These differences in method, pace and tradition are a great misfortune to the whole English-speaking world. We English people do not respect Americans enough; we are too disposed to think they are all Quincy Howes and Harry Elmer Barneses and Borahs and suchlike, conceited and suspicious anti-British monomaniacs, who must be humoured at any cost; which is why we are never so frank and rude with them as they deserve. But the more we must contain ourselves the less we love them. Real brothers can curse each other and keep friends. Someday Britannia will give Columbia a piece of her mind, and that may clear the air. Said an exasperated Englishman to me a day or so ago: "I pray to God they keep out of the end of this war anyhow. We shall never hear the last of it if they don't. . . ."

Yet at a different pace our two people are travelling towards identical ends, and it is lamentable that a difference of accent and idiom should do more mischief than a difference of language.

So far as Great Britain goes things are nearer and closer to me, and it seems to me that there is an excellent opportunity now to catch the country in a state of socialisation and suspend party politics, and keep it at that. It is a logical but often disregarded corollary of the virtual creation of All-Party National Governments and suspension of electoral contests, that since there is no Opposition, party criticism should give place to individual criticism of ministers, and instead of throwing out governments we should set ourselves to throw out individual administrative failures. We need no longer confine our choice of public servants to political careerists. We can insist upon men who have done things and can do things, and whenever an election occurs we can organise a block of non-party voters who will vote it possible for an outsider of proved ability, and will at any rate insist on a clear statement from every Parliamentary candidate of the concrete service, if any, he has done the country, of his past and present financial entanglements and his family relationships and of any title he possesses. We can get these necessary particulars published and note what newspapers decline to do so. And if there are still only politicians to vote for, we can at least vote and spoil our voting cards by way of protest.

At present we see one public service after another in a mess through the incompetent handling of some party hack and the unseen activities of interested parties. People are asking already why Sir Arthur Salter is not in control of Allied Shipping again, Sir John Orr directing our food supply with perhaps Sir Fredrick Keeble to help him, Sir Robert Vansittart in the Foreign Office. We want to know the individuals responsible for the incapacity of our Intelligence and Propaganda Ministries, so that we may induce them to quit public life. It would be quite easy now to excite a number of anxious people with a cry for "Competence not Party".

Most people in the British Isles are heartily sick of Mr Chamberlain and his government, but they cannot face up to a political split in wartime, and Mr Chamberlain sticks to office with all the pertinacity of a Barnacle. But if we do not attack the government as a whole, but individual ministers, and if we replace them one by one, we shall presently have a government so rejuvenated that even Mr Chamberlain will realise and accept his superannuation. Quite a small body of public-spirited people could organise an active Vigilance Society to

99

keep these ideas before the mass of voters and begin the elimination of inferior elements from our public life. This would be a practical job of primary importance in our political regeneration. It would lead directly to a new and more efficient political structure to carry on after the present war has collapsed or otherwise ended.

Following upon this campaign for the conclusive interment of the played-out party system, there comes the necessity for a much more strenuous search for administrative and technical ability throughout the country. We do not want to miss a single youngster who can be of use in the great business of making over Great Britain, which has been so rudely, clumsily and wastefully socialised by our war perturbations, so that it may become a permanently efficient system.

And from the base of the educational pyramid up to its apex of higher education of teachers, heads of departments and research, there is need for such a quickening of minds and methods as only a more or less organised movement of sanely critical men can bring about. We want ministers now of the highest quality in every department, but in no department of public life is a man of creative understanding, bold initiative and administrative power so necessary as in the Education Ministry.

So tranquil and unobtrusive has been the flow of educational affairs in the British Empire that it seems almost scandalous, and it is certainly "vulgar", to suggest that we need an educational Ginger Group to discover and support such a minister. We want a Minister of Education who can shock teachers into self-examination, electrify and rejuvenate old dons or put them away in ivory towers, and stimulate the

younger ones. Under the party system the Education Ministry
has always been a restful corner for some deserving party
politician with an abject respect for his Alma Mater and the
permanent officials. During war time, when other departments
wake up, the Education Department sinks into deeper lethargy.
One cannot recall a single British Education Minister, since
there have been such things in our island story as Ministers for
Education, who signified anything at all educationally or did
anything of his own impulse that was in the least worth while.

Suppose we found a live one - soon - and let him rip!

There again is something to be done far more revolutionary
than throwing bombs at innocent policemen or assassinating
harmless potentates or ex-potentates. And yet it is only asking
that an existing department be what it pretends to be.

A third direction in which any gathering accumulation of sanity
should direct its attention is the clumsy unfairness and
indirectness of our present methods of expropriating the former
well-to-do classes. The only observable principle seems to be
widows and children first. Socialisation is being effected in
Britain and America alike not by frank expropriation (with or
without compensation) but by increasing government control
and increasing taxation. Both our great communities are going
into socialism backward and without ever looking round. This
is good in so far as that technical experience and directive
ability is changed over step by step from entirely private
employment to public service, and on that side sane and helpful
citizens have little to do beyond making the process conscious
of itself and the public aware of the real nature of the change,
but it is bad in its indiscriminate destruction of savings, which
are the most exposed and vulnerable side of the old system.

101

They are expropriated by profit-control and taxation alike, and at the same time they suffer in purchasing power by the acceleration of that process of monetary inflation which is the unavoidable readjustment, the petition in bankruptcy, of a community that has overspent.

The shareholding class dwindles and dies; widows and orphans, the old who are past work and the infirm who are incapable of it, are exposed in their declining years to a painful shrinkage of their modes of living; there is no doubt a diminution of social waste, but also there is an indirect impoverishment of free opinion and free scientific and artistic initiative as the endless societies, institutions and services which have enriched life for us and been very largely supported by voluntary subscriptions, shrivel. At present a large proportion of our scientific, artistic, literary and social workers are educated out of the private savings fund. In a class-war revolution these economically very defenceless but socially very convenient people are subjected to vindictive humiliation - it is viewed as a great triumph for their meaner neighbours - but a revolution sanely conducted will probably devise a system of terminable annuities and compensation, and of assistance to once voluntary associations, which will ease off the social dislocations due to the disappearance of one stratum of relatively free and independent people, before its successors, that is to say the growing class of retired officials, public administrators and so forth, find their feet and develop their own methods of assertion and enterprise.

Chapter 10

Declaration of the Rights of Man

Let us turn now to another system of problems in the collectivisation of the world, and that is the preservation of liberty in the socialist state and the restoration of that confidence without which good behaviour is generally impossible.

This destruction of confidence is one of the less clearly recognised evils of the present phase of world-disintegration. In the past there have been periods when whole communities or at least large classes within communities have gone about their business with a general honesty, directness and sense of personal honour. They have taken a keen pride in the quality of their output. They have lived through life on tolerable and tolerant terms with their neighbours. The laws they observed have varied in different countries and periods, but their general nature was to make an orderly law-abiding life possible and natural. They had been taught and they believed and they had every reason to believe: "This (that or the other thing) is right. Do right and nothing, except by some strange exceptional misfortune, can touch you. The Law guarantees you that. Do right and nothing will rob you or frustrate you."

Nowhere in the world now is there very much of that feeling left, and as it disappears, the behaviour of people degenerates towards a panic scramble, towards cheating, over-reaching, gang organisation, precautionary hoarding, concealment and all the meanness and anti-social feeling which is the natural outcome of insecurity.

Faced with what now amounts to something like a moral stampede, more and more sane men will realise the urgency for a restoration of confidence. The more socialisation proceeds and the more directive authority is concentrated, the more necessary is an efficient protection of individuals from the impatience of well-meaning or narrow-minded or ruthless officials and indeed from all the possible abuses of advantage that are inevitable under such circumstances to our still childishly wicked breed.

In the past the Atlantic world has been particularly successful in expedients for meeting this aspect of human nature. Our characteristic and traditional method may be called the method of the fundamental declaration. Our Western peoples, by a happy instinct, have produced statements of Right, from Magna Carta onwards, to provide a structural defence between the citizen and the necessary growth of central authority.

And plainly the successful organisation of the more universal and penetrating collectivism that is now being forced upon us all, will be frustrated in its most vital aspect unless its organisation is accompanied by the preservative of a new Declaration of the Rights of Man, that must, because of the increasing complexity of the social structure, be more generous, detailed and explicit than any of its predecessors. Such a Declaration must become the common fundamental law of all communities and collectivities assembled under the World Pax. It should be interwoven with the declared war aims

of the combatant powers now; it should become the primary
fact in any settlement; it should be put before the now
combatant states for their approval, their embarrassed silence
or their rejection.

In order to be as clear as possible about this, let me submit a
draft for your consideration of this proposed Declaration of the
Rights of Man - using "man" of course to cover every
individual, male or female, of the species. I have endeavoured
to bring in everything that is essential and to omit whatever
secondary issues can be easily deduced from its general
statements. It is a draft for your consideration. Points may have
been overlooked and it may contain repetitions and superfluous
statements.

"Since a man comes into this world through no fault of his
own, since he is manifestly a joint inheritor of the
accumulations of the past, and since those accumulations are
more than sufficient to justify the claims that are here made for
him, it follows:

"(1) That every man without distinction of race, of colour or of
professed belief or opinions, is entitled to the nourishment,
covering, medical care and attention needed to realise his full
possibilities of physical and mental development and to keep
him in a state of health from his birth to death.

"(2) That he is entitled to sufficient education to make him a
useful and interested citizen, that special education should be
so made available as to give him equality of opportunity for the
development of his distinctive gifts in the service of mankind,
that he should have easy access to information upon all matters

of common knowledge throughout his life and enjoy the utmost freedom of discussion, association and worship.

"(3) That he may engage freely in any lawful occupation, earning such pay as the need for his work and the increment it makes to the common welfare may justify. That he is entitled to paid employment and to a free choice whenever there is any variety of employment open to him. He may suggest employment for himself and have his claim publicly considered, accepted or dismissed.

"(4) That he shall have the right to buy or sell without any discriminatory restrictions anything which may be lawfully bought or sold, in such quantities and with such reservations as are compatible with the common welfare."

(Here I will interpolate a comment. We have to bear in mind that in a collectivist state buying and selling to secure income and profit will be not simply needless but impossible. The Stock Exchange, after its career of four-hundred-odd-years, will necessarily vanish with the disappearance of any rational motive either for large accumulations or for hoarding against deprivation and destitution. Long before the age of complete collectivisation arrives, the savings of individuals for later consumption will probably be protected by some development of the Unit Trust System into a public service. They will probably be entitled to interest at such a rate as to compensate for that secular inflation which should go on in a steadily enriched world community. Inheritance and bequest in a community in which the means of production and of all possible monopolisation are collectivised, can concern little else than relatively small, beautiful and intimate objects, which will afford pleasure but no unfair social advantage to the receiver.)

"(5) That he and his personal property lawfully acquired are entitled to police and legal protection from private violence, deprivation, compulsion and intimidation.

"(6) That he may move freely about the world at his own expense. That his private house or apartment or reasonably limited garden enclosure is his castle, which may be entered only with consent, but that he shall have the right to come and go over any kind of country, moorland, mountain, farm, great garden or what not, or upon the seas, lakes and rivers of the world, where his presence will not be destructive of some special use, dangerous to himself nor seriously inconvenient to his fellow-citizens.

"(7) That a man unless he is declared by a competent authority to be a danger to himself and to others through mental abnormality, a declaration which must be annually confirmed, shall not be imprisoned for a longer period than six days without being charged with a definite offence against the law, nor for more than three months without public trial. At the end if the latter period, if he has not been tried and sentenced by due process of law, he shall be released. Nor shall he be conscripted for military, police or any other service to which he has a conscientious objection.

"(8) That although a man is subject to the free criticism of his fellows, he shall have adequate protection from any lying or misrepresentation that may distress or injure him. All administrative registration and records about a man shall be open to his personal and private inspection. There shall be no secret dossiers in any administrative department. All dossiers shall be accessible to the man concerned and subject to verification and correction at his challenge. A dossier is merely a memorandum; it cannot be used as evidence without proper confirmation in open court.

"(9) That no man shall be subjected to any sort of mutilation or sterilisation except with his own deliberate consent, freely given, nor to bodily assault, except in restraint of his own violence, nor to torture, beating or any other bodily punishment; he shall not be subjected to imprisonment with such an excess of silence, noise, light or darkness as to cause mental suffering, or to imprisonment in infected, verminous or otherwise insanitary quarters, or be put into the company of verminous or infectious people. He shall not be forcibly fed nor prevented from starving himself if he so desire. He shall not be forced to take drugs nor shall they be administered to him without his knowledge and consent. That the extreme punishments to which he may be subjected are rigorous imprisonment for a term of not longer than fifteen years or death."

(Here I would point out that there is nothing in this to prevent any country from abolishing the death penalty any country from abolishing the death penalty. Nor do I assert a general right to commit suicide, because no one can punish a man for doing that. He has escaped. But threats and incompetent attempts to commit suicide belong to an entirely different category. They are indecent and distressing acts that can easily become a serious social nuisance, from which the normal citizen is entitled to protection.)

"(10) That the provisions and principles embodied in this Declaration shall be more fully defined in a code of fundamental human rights which shall be made easily accessible to everyone. This Declaration shall not be qualified nor departed from upon any pretext whatever. It incorporates all previous Declarations of Human Right. Henceforth for a new ear it is the fundamental law for mankind throughout the whole world.

"No treaty and no law affecting these primary rights shall be binding upon any man or province or administrative division of the community, that has not been made openly, by and with the active or tacit acquiescence of every adult citizen concerned, either given by a direct majority vote of his publicly elected representatives. In matters of collective behaviour it is by the majority decision men must abide. No administration, under a pretext of urgency, convenience or the like, shall be entrusted with powers to create or further define offences or set up by-laws, which will in any way infringe the rights and liberties here asserted. All legislation must be public and definite. No secret treaties shall be binding on individuals, organisations or communities. No orders in council or the like, which extend the application of a law, shall be permitted. There is no source of law but the people, and since life flows on constantly to new citizens, no generation of the people can in whole or in part surrender or delegate the legislative power inherent in mankind."

There, I think, is something that keener minds than mine may polish into a working Declaration which would in the most effective manner begin that restoration of confidence of which the world stands in need. Much of it might be better phrased, but I think it embodies the general good-will in mankind from

109

pole to pole. It is certainly what we all want for ourselves. It could be a very potent instrument indeed in the present phase of human affairs. It is necessary and it is acceptable. Incorporate that in your peace treaties and articles of federation, I would say, and you will have a firm foundation, which will continually grow firmer, for the fearless cosmopolitan life of a new world order. You will never get that order without some such document. It is the missing key to endless contemporary difficulties.

And if we, the virtuous democracies, are not fighting for these common human rights, then what in the name of the nobility and gentry, the Crown and the Established Church, the City, The Times and the Army and Navy Club, are we common British peoples fighting for?

Chapter 11

International Politics

And now, having completed our picture of what the saner
elements in human society may reasonably work for and hope
for, having cleared away the horrible nightmares of the class
war and the totalitarian slave-state from our imaginations, we
are able to attack the immediate riddles of international conflict
and relationship with some hope of a general solution. If we
realise to the depths of our being that a world settlement based
in the three ideas of socialism, law and knowledge, is not only
possible and desirable, but the only way of escape from
deepening disaster, then manifestly our attitude towards the
resentments of Germany, the prejudices of America or Russia,
the poverty and undernourishment of India or the ambitions of
Japan, must be frankly opportunist. None of these are primary
issues. We sane men must never lose sight of our ultimate
objective, but our methods of getting there will have to vary
with the fluctuating variations of national feeling and national
policy.

There is this idea of federalism upon which I have already
submitted a criticism in chapter seven. As I have shown there,
the Streit proposals will either take you further or land you
nowhere. Let us assume that we can strengthen his proposals to
the extent of making a socialistic economic consortium and
adhesion to that Declaration of Rights, primary conditions for

any federal union; then it becomes a matter of mood and occasion with what communities the federal association may be begun. We can even encourage feeble federal experiments which do not venture even so far as that along the path to sanity, in the certainty that either they will fade out again or else that they will become liberal realities of the type to which the whole world must ultimately conform. Behind any such half-hearted tentatives an educational propaganda can be active and effective.

But when it comes to the rate and amount of participation in the construction of a rational world order we can expect from any country or group of countries, we are in a field where there is little more than guessing and haphazard generalisations about "national character" to work upon. We are dealing with masses of people which may be swayed enormously by a brilliant newspaper or an outstandingly persuasive or compelling personality or by almost accidental changes in the drift of events. I, for example, cannot tell how far the generality of educated and capable people in the British Empire now may fall in with our idea of accepting and serving a collectivism, or how strong their conservative resistance may be. It is my own country and I ought to know it best, and I do not know it detachedly enough or deeply enough to decide that. I do not see how anyone can foretell these swirls and eddies of response.

The advocacy of such movements of the mind and will as I am speaking of here is in itself among the operating causes in political adjustment, and those who are deepest in the struggle are least able to estimate how it is going. Every factor in political and international affairs is a fluctuating factor. The wise man therefore will not set his heart upon any particular drift or combination. He will favour everything that trends towards the end at which he aims.

The present writer cherishes the idea that the realisation of a common purpose and a common cultural inheritance may spread throughout all the English-speaking communities, and there can be no harm in efforts to give this concrete expression. He believes the dissociation of the British Empire may inaugurate this great synthesis. At the same time there are factors making for some closer association of the United States of America with what are called the Oslo powers. There is no reason why one of these associations should stand in the way of the other. Some countries such as Canada rest already under what is practically a double guarantee; she has the security of the Monroe Doctrine and the protection of the British fleet.

A Germany of eighty million people which has been brought to acquiesce in the Declaration of the Rights of Man and which is already highly collectivised, may come much earlier to a completely liberal socialist regime than Great Britain or France. If she participates in a consortium for the development of what are called the politically backward regions of the world, she may no longer be disposed for further military adventures and further stress and misery. She may enter upon a phase of social and economic recovery so rapid as to stimulate and react upon every other country in the world. It is not for other countries to dictate her internal politics, and if the German people want to remain united as one people, in federated states or in one centralised state, there is neither righteousness nor wisdom preventing them.

The Germans like the rest of the world have to get on with collectivisation, they have to produce their pattern, and they

113

cannot give themselves to that if they are artificially divided up and disorganised by some old-fashioned Quai d'Orsay scheme. They must do the right thing in their own way.

That the belligerent tradition may linger on in Germany for a generation or so, is a risk the Atlantic powers have to take. The world has a right to insist that not simply some German government but the people generally, recognise unequivocally and repeatedly, the rights of man asserted in the Declaration, and it is disarmed and that any aggressive plant, any war plane, warship, gun or arsenal that is discovered in the country shall be destroyed forthwith, brutally and completely. But that is a thing that should not be confined to Germany. Germany should not be singled out for that. Armament should be an illegality everywhere, and some sort of international force should patrol a treaty-bound world. Partial armament is one of those absurdities dear to moderate-minded "reasonable" men. Armament itself is making war. Making a gun, pointing a gun and firing it, are all acts of the same order. It should be illegal to construct anywhere upon earth, any mechanism for the specific purpose of killing men. When you see a gun it is reasonable to ask: "Whom is that intended to kill?"

Germany's rearmament after 1918 was largely tolerated because she played off British Russophobia against the Russian fear of "Capitalist" attack, but that excuse can no longer serve any furtive war-mongers among her people after her pact with Moscow.

Released from the economic burdens and restrictions that crippled her recovery after 1918, Germany may find a full and satisfying outlet for the energy of her young men in her systematic collectivisation, raising the standard of her common life deliberately and steadily, giving Russia a lead in efficiency and obliging the maundering "politics" and discursive inattention of the Atlantic world to remain concentrated upon the realities of life. The idea of again splitting up Germany into discordant fragments so as to postpone her ultimate recovery indefinitely, is a pseudo-democratic slacker's dream. It is diametrically opposed to world reconstruction. We have need of the peculiar qualities of her people, and the sooner she recovers the better for the whole world. It is preposterous to resume the policy of holding back Germany simply that the old order may enjoy a few more years of self-indulgence in England, France and America.

A lingering fear of German military aggression may not be altogether bad for the minor states of South-Eastern Europe and Asia Minor, by breaking down their excessive nationalism and inducing them to work together. The policy of the sane man should be to welcome every possible experiment in international understandings duplicate and overlap one another, so much the better. He has to watch the activities of his own Foreign Office with incessant jealousy, for signs of that Machiavellian spirit which foments division among foreign governments and peoples and schemes perpetually to frustrate the progressive movement in human affairs by converting it into a swaying indecisive balance of power.

This book is a discussion of guiding principles and not of the endless specific problems of adjustment that arise on the way to a world realisation of collective unity. I will merely glance at that old idea of Napoleon the Third's, the Latin Union, at the possibility of a situation in Spanish and Portuguese South America parallel to that overlap of the Monroe Doctrine and the European motherlands which already exists in practice in

115

the case of Canada, nor will I expatiate upon the manifold possibilities of sincere application of the Declaration of the Rights of Man to India and Africa - and particularly to those parts of the world in which more or less black peoples are awakening to the realities of racial discrimination and oppression.

I will utter a passing warning against any Machiavellian treatment of the problem of Northern and Eastern Asia, into which the British may be led by their constitutional Russophobia. The Soviet collectivism, especially if presently it becomes liberalised and more efficient through a recovery from its present obsession by Stalin, may spread very effectively across Central Asia and China. To anyone nourished mentally upon the ideas of an unending competition of Powers for ascendancy for ever and ever, an alliance with Japan, as truculent and militarised a Japan as possible, will seem the most natural response in the world. But to anyone who has grasped the reality of the present situation of mankind and the urgent desirableness of world collectivisation, this immense unification will be something to welcome, criticise and assist.

The old bugbear of Russia's "designs upon India" may also play its part in distorting the Asiatic situation for many people. Yet a hundred years of mingled neglect, exploitation and occasional outbreaks of genuine helpfulness should have taught the British that the ultimate fate of India's hundreds of millions rests now upon no conquering ruler but wholly and solely upon the ability of the Indian peoples to co-operate in world collectivisation. They may learn much by way of precept and example from Russia and from the English-speaking world, but the days for mere revolt or for relief by a change of masters have passed. India has to work out for itself, with its own manner of participation in the struggle for a world order, starting from the British raj as a datum line. No outside power can work that out for the Indian peoples, nor force them to do it if they have no will for it.

But I will not wander further among these ever-changing problems and possibilities. They are, so to speak, wayside eventualities and opportunities. Immense though some of them are they remain secondary. Every year or so now the shifting channels of politics need to be recharted. The activities and responses of the sane man in any particular country and at any particular time will be determined always by the overruling conception of a secular movement towards a single world order. That will be the underlying permanent objective of all his political life.

There is, however, another line of world consolidation to which attention must be drawn before we conclude this section, and is what we may call ad hoc internationalism is admirably set forth in Leonard Woolf's International Government, a classic which was published in 1916 and still makes profitable reading.

The typical ad hoc organisation is the Postal Union, which David Lubin, that brilliant neglected thinker, would have had extended until it controlled shipping and equalised freights throughout the world. He based his ideas upon his practical experience of the mail order business from which he derived his very considerable fortune. From that problem of freight adjustment he passed to the idea of a controlled survey of world, so that a shortage here or a glut there could be foreseen and remedied in time. He realised the idea in the form of the International Institute of Agriculture at Rome, which in its heyday made treaties like an independent sovereign power for the supply of returns from nearly every government upon earth. The war of 1914 and Lubin's death in 1919 checked the development of this admirable and most inspiring experiment in ad hoc internationalism. Its history is surely something that should be made part of the compulsory education of every statesmen and publicist. Yet never in my life have I met a professional politician who knew anything whatever or wanted to know anything about it. It didn't get votes; it seemed difficult to tax it; what was the good of it?

Another ad hoc organisation which might be capable of a considerable extension of its functions is the Elder Brethren of Trinity House, who control the lighthouses and charting of the seas throughout the world. But it would need a very considerable revision and extension of Mr Woolf's book and, in spite of the war stresses that have delayed and in some cases reversed their development, it would be quite beyond our present scope, to bring up to date the lengthening tale of ad hoc international networks, ranging from international business cartels, scientific and technical organisations, white-slave-trade suppression and international police co-operation, to health services and religious missions. Just as I have suggested that the United States and Great Britain may become complete socialisms unawares, so it is a not altogether impossible dream that the world may discover to its great surprise that it is already practically a cosmopolis, through the extension and interweaving of these ad hoc co-operations. At any rate we have this very powerful collateral process going on side by side with the more definite political schemes we have discussed.

Surveying the possibilities of these various attacks upon the complicated and intricate obstacles that stand between us and a new and more hopeful world order, one realises both the reasons for hope in that great possibility and the absurdity over over-confidence. We are all like soldiers upon a vast battlefield; we cannot be sure of the trend of things; we may be elated when disillusionment is rushing headlong upon us; we may be on the verge of despair, not knowing that our antagonists are already in collapse. My own reactions vary between an almost mystical faith in the ultimate triumph of human reason and good-will, and moods of stoical determination to carry on to the end in the face of what looks like inevitable disaster. There are quantitative factors in the outlook for which there are no data; there are elements of time and opportunity beyond any estimating. Every one of these activities we have been canvassing tends to delay the drift to destruction and provides a foothold for a further counter-offensive against the adversary.

In the companion predecessor to this book, The Fate of Homo sapiens, I tried to drive home the fact that our species has no more reason to believe it can escape defeat and extinction, than any other organism that plays or has played its part in the drama of life. I tried to make clear how precarious is our present situation, and how urgent it is that we should make a strenuous effort at adjustment now. Only a little while ago it seemed as though that was an appeal to a deaf and blind world, invincibly set in its habitual ways into the question whether this inclination towards pessimism reflected a mood or phase in myself, and I threw out a qualifying suggestion or so; but for my own part I could not find any serious reason to believe that the mental effort that was clearly necessary if man was to escape that fate that marched upon him would ever be made. His conservative resistances, his apathy, seemed incurable.

H. G. Wells

Now suddenly everywhere one meets with alarmed and open and enquiring minds. So far the tremendous dislocations of the present war have been immensely beneficial in stripping off what seemed to be quite invincible illusions of security only a year ago. I never expected to live to see the world with its eyes as widely open as they are to-day. The world has never been so awake. Little may come of it, much may come of it. We do not know. Life would amount to nothing at all if we did.

Chapter 12

World Order in Being

There will be no day of days then when a new world order comes into being. Step by step and here and there it will arrive, and even as it comes into being it will develop fresh perspectives, discover unsuspected problems and go on to new adventures. No man, no group of men, will ever be singled out as its father or founder. For its maker will be not this man nor that man nor any man but Man, that being who is in some measure in every one of us. World order will be, like science, like most inventions, a social product, an innumerable number of personalities will have lived fine lives, pouring their best into the collective achievement.

We can find a small-scale parallel to the probable development of a new world order in the history of flying. Less than a third of a century ago, ninety-nine people out of a hundred would have told you that flying was impossible; kites and balloons and possibly even a navigable balloon, they could imagine; they had known of such things for a hundred years; but a heavier then air machine, flying in defiance of wind and gravity! That they knew was nonsense. The would-be aviator was the typical comic inventor. Any fool could laugh at him. Now consider how completely the air is conquered.

And who did it? Nobody and everybody. Twenty thousand
brains or so, each contributing a notion, a device, an
amplification. They stimulated one another; they took off from
one another. They were like excited ganglia in a larger brain
sending their impulses to and fro. They were people of the
most diverse race and colour. You can write down perhaps a
hundred people or so who have figured conspicuously in the
air, and when you examine the rôle they have played, you will
find for the most part that they are mere notorieties of the
Lindbergh type who have put themselves modestly but firmly
in the limelight and can lay no valid claim to any effective
contribution whatever. You will find many disputes about
records and priority in making this or that particular step, but
the lines of suggestion, the growth and elaboration of the idea,
have been an altogether untraceable process. It has been going
on for not more than a third of a century, under our very eyes,
and no one can say precisely how it came about. One man said
"Why not this?" and tried it, and another said "Why not that?"
A vast miscellany of people had one idea in common, an idea
as old as Dædalus, the idea that "Man can fly". Suddenly,
swiftly, it got about - that is the only phrase you can use - that
flying was attainable. And man, man as a social being, turned
his mind to it seriously, and flew.

So it will certainly be with the new world order, if ever it is
attained. A growing miscellany of people are saying - it is
getting about - that "World Pax is possible", a World Pax in
which men will be both united and free and creative. It is of no
importance at all that nearly every man of fifty and over
receives the idea with a pitying smile. Its chief dangers are the
dogmatist and the would-be "leader" who will try to suppress
every collateral line of work which does not minister to his
supremacy. This movement must be, and it must remain, many-

headed. Suppose the world had decided that Santos Dumont or Hiram Maxim was the heaven-sent Master of the Air, had given him the right to appoint a successor and subjected all experiments to his inspired control. We should probably have the Air Master now, with an applauding retinue of yes-men, following the hops of some clumsy, useless and extremely dangerous apparatus across country with the utmost dignity and self-satisfaction . . . .

Yet that is precisely how we still set about our political and social problems.

Bearing this essential fact in mind that the Peace of Man can only be attained, if it is attained at all, by an advance upon a long and various front, at varying speed and with diverse equipment, keeping direction only by a common faith in the triple need for collectivism, law and research, we realise the impossibility of drawing any picture of the new order as though it was as settled and stable as the old order imagined itself to be. The new order will be incessant; things will never stop happening, and so it defies any Utopian description. But we may nevertheless assemble a number of possibilities that will be increasingly realisable as the tide of disintegration ebbs and the new order is revealed.

To begin with we have to realise certain peculiarities of human behaviour that are all too disregarded in general political speculation. We have considered the very important rôle that may be played in our contemporary difficulties by a clear statement of the Rights of Man, and we have sketched such a Declaration. There is not an item in that Declaration, I believe, which a man will not consider to be a reasonable demand - so far as he himself is concerned. He will subscribe to it in that spirit very readily. But when he is asked not only to concede by the same gesture to everybody else in the world, but as something for which he has to make all the sacrifices necessary for its practical realisation, he will discover a reluctance to "go so far as that". He will find a serious resistance welling up from his sub-conscious and trying to justify itself in his thoughts.

The things he will tell you will be very variable; but the word "premature" will play a large part in it. He will display a tremendous tenderness and consideration with which you have never credited him before, for servants, for workers, for aliens and particularly for aliens of a different colour from himself. They will hurt themselves with all this dangerous liberty. Are they fit, he will ask you, for all this freedom? "Candidly, are they fit for it?" He will be slightly offended if you will say, "As fit as you are". He will say in a slightly amused tone, "But how can you say that?" and then going off rather at a tangent, "I am afraid you idealise your fellow-creatures."

As you press him, you will find this kindliness evaporating from his resistance altogether. He is now concerned about the general beauty and loveliness of the world. He will protest that this new Magna Carta will reduce all the world to "a dead level of uniformity". You will ask him why must a world of free-men be uniform and at a dead level? You will get no adequate reply. It is an assumption of vital importance to him and he must cling to it. He has been accustomed to associate "free" and "equal", and has never been bright-minded enough to take these two words apart and have a good look at them separately. He is likely to fall back at this stage upon that Bible of the impotent genteel, Huxley's Brave New World, and implore you to read it. You brush that disagreeable fantasy aside and continue to press him. He says that nature has made men unequal, and you reply that that is no reason for exaggerating the fact. The more unequal and various their gifts, the greater is the necessity for a Magna Carta to protect them from one another. Then he will talk of robbing life of the picturesque and the romantic and you will have some difficulty in getting these words defined. Sooner or later it will grow clear that he finds the prospect of a world in which "Jack's as good as his Master" unpleasant to the last degree.

If you still probe him with questions and leading suggestions, you will begin to realise how large a part the need for glory over his fellows plays in his composition (and incidentally you will note, please, you own secret satisfaction in carrying the argument against him). It will become clear to you, if you collate the specimen under examination with the behaviour of children, yourself and the people about you, under what urgent necessity they are for the sense of triumph, of being better and doing better than their fellows, and having it felt and recognised by someone. It is a deeper, steadier impulse than sexual lust; it is a hunger. It is the clue to the unlovingness of so much sexual life, to sadistic impulses, to avarice, hoarding and endless ungainful cheating and treachery which gives men the sense of getting the better of someone even if they do not get the upper hand.

In the last resort this is why we must have law, and why Magna Carta and all its kindred documents set out to defeat human nature in defence of the general happiness. Law is essentially an adjustment of that craving to glory over other living things, to the needs of social life, and it is more necessary in a collectivist society than in any other. It is a bargain, it is a social contract, to do as we would be done by and to repress our extravagant egotisms in return for reciprocal concessions.

And in the face of these considerations we have advanced about the true nature of the beast we have to deal with, it is plain that the politics of the sane man as we have reasoned them out, must anticipate a strenuous opposition to this primary vital implement for bringing about the new world order.

I have suggested that the current discussion of "War Aims" may very effectively be transformed into the propaganda of this new Declaration of the Rights of Man. The opposition to it and the attempts that will be made to postpone, mitigate, stifle and evade it, need to be watched, denounced and combatted persistently throughout the world. I do not know how far this Declaration I have sketched can be accepted by a good Catholic, but the Totalitarian pseudo-philosophy insists upon inequality of treatment for "non-Aryans" as a glorious duty. How Communists would respond to its clauses would, I suppose, depend upon their orders from Moscow. But what are called the "democracies" are supposed to be different, and it would be possible now to make that Declaration a searching test of the honesty and spirit of the leaders and rulers in whom they trust. These rulers can be brought to the point by it, with a precision unattainable in any other fashion.

But the types and characters and authorities and officials and arrogant and aggressive individuals who will boggle at this Declaration and dispute and defy it, do not exhaust the resistances of our unregenerate natures to this implement for the establishment of elementary justice in the world. For a far larger proportion of people among the "democracies" will be found, who will pay it lip service and then set about discovering how, in their innate craving for that sense of superiority and advantage which lies so near the core of our individuals wills, they may unobtrusively sabotage it and cheat it. Even if they only cheat it just a little. I am inclined to think this disingenuousness is a universal weakness. I have a real passion for serving the world, but I have a pretty keen disposition to get more pay for my service, more recognition and so on than I deserve. I do not trust myself. I want to be under just laws. We want law because we are all potential law-breakers.

This is a considerable digression into psychology, and I will do no more than glance at how large a part this craving for superiority and mastery has played in the sexual practices of mankind. There we have the ready means for a considerable relief of this egotistical tension in mutual boasting and reassurance. But the motive for his digression here is to emphasise the fact that the generalisation of our "War Aims" into a Declaration of Rights, though it will enormously simplify the issue of the war, will eliminate neither open and heartfelt opposition nor endless possibilities of betrayal and sabotage.

Nor does it alter the fact that even when the struggle seems to be drifting definitely towards a world social democracy, there may still be very great delays and disappointments before it becomes an efficient and beneficent world system. Countless people, from maharajas to millionaires and from pukkha sahibs to pretty ladies, will hate the new world order, be rendered unhappy by frustration of their passions and ambitions through its advent and will die protesting against it. When we attempt to estimate its promise we have to bear in mind the distress of a generation or so of malcontents, many of them quite gallant and graceful-looking people.

Ant it will be no light matter to minimise the loss of efficiency in the process of changing the spirit and pride of administration work from that of an investing, high-salaried man with a handsome display of expenditure and a socially ambitious wife, into a relatively less highly-salaried man with a higher standard of self-criticism, aware that he will be esteemed rather by what he puts into his work than by what he gets out of it. There will be a lot of social spill, tragi-comedy and loss of efficiency during the period of the change over, and it is better to be prepared for that.

Yet after making allowances for these transitional stresses we may still look forward with some confidence to certain phases in the onset of World Order. War or war fear will have led everywhere to the concentration of vast numbers of workers upon munition work and the construction of offensive and defensive structures of all sorts, upon shipping, internal communications, replacement structures, fortification. There will be both a great accumulation and control of material and constructive machinery and also of hands already growing accustomed to handling it. As the possibility of conclusive victory fades and this war muddle passes out of its distinctively military phase towards revolution, and as some sort of Peace Congress assembles, it will be not only desirable but necessary for governments to turn over these resources and activities to social reconstruction. It will be too obviously dangerous and wasteful to put them out of employment. They must surely have learnt now what unemployment means in terms of social disorganisation. Governments will have to lay out the world, plan and build for peace whether they like it or not.

But it will be asked, "Where will you find the credit to do that?" and to answer this question we must reiterate that fact that money is an expedient and not an end. The world will have the material and the hands needed for a reconditioning of its life everywhere. They are all about you now crying out to be used. It is, or at any rate it has been, the function of the contemporary money-credit system to bring worker and material together and stimulate their union. That system always justified its activities on that ground, that is its claim to exist, and if it does not exist for that purpose then for what purpose does it exist and what further need is there for it? If now the financial mechanism will not work, if it confronts us with a non possumus, then clearly it resigns its function.

Then it has to get out of the way. It will declare the world has stopped when the truth will be that the City has stopped. It is the counting-house that has gone bankrupt. For a long time now an increasing number of people have been asking questions about the world counting-house, getting down at last to such fundamental questions as "What is money?" and "Why are Banks?" It is disconcerting but stimulating to find that no lucid answer is forthcoming.

One might have imagined that long before this one of the many great bankers and financial experts in our world would have come forward with a clear and simple justification for the monetary practices of to-day. He would have shown how completely reasonable and trustworthy this money-credit system was. He would have shown what was temporarily wrong with it and how to set it working again, as the electrician does when the lights go out. He would have released us from our deepening distress about our money in the Bank, our little squirrel hoard of securities, the deflating lifebelt of property that was to assure our independence to the end. No one of that quality comes forward. There is not so much as a latter-day

129

Bagehot. It dawns upon more and more of us that it is not a system at all and never has been a system, that it is an accumulation of conventions, usages, collateral developments and compensatory expedients, which creaks now and sways more and more and gives every sign of a complete and horrifying social collapse.

Most of us have believed up to the last moment that somewhere distributed among the banks and city offices in a sort of world counting-house, there were books of accounts, multitudinous perhaps and intricate, but ultimately proper accounts. Only now is it dawning upon comfortable decent people that the counting-house is in a desperate mess, that codes seem to have been lost, entries made wrong, additions gone astray down the column, records kept in vanishing ink. . .
.

For years there has been a great and growing literature about money. It is very various but it has one general characteristic. First there is a swift exposure of the existing system as wrong. Then there is a glib demonstration of a new system which is right. Let this be done or that be done, "let the nation own its own money", says one radio prophet earnestly, repeatedly, simply, and all will be well. These various systems of doctrine run periodicals, organise movements (with coloured shirt complete), meet, demonstrate. They disregard each other flatly. And without exception all these monetary reformers betray signs of extreme mental strain.

The secret trouble in their minds is gnawing doubt that their own proper "plan", the panacea, is in some subtle and treacherous way likely to fail them if it is put to the test. The internal fight against this intolerable shadow betrays itself in their outer behaviour. Their letters and pamphlets, with scarcely an exception, have this much in common with the letters one gets from lunatics, that there is a continual resort to capital letters and abusive terms. They shout out at the slightest provocation or none. They are not so much shouting at the exasperating reader who remains so obstinate when they have been so clear, so clear, as at the sceptical whisper within.

Because there is no perfect money system by itself and there never can be. It is a dream like the elixir vitæ or perpetual motion. It is in the same order of thought.

Attention has already been drawn, in our examination of Mr Streit's proposals for Union Now, to the fact that money varies in its nature and operations with the theory of property and distribution on which society is based, that in a complete collectivism for example it becomes little more than the check handed to the worker to enable him to purchase whatever he likes from the resources of the community. Every detachment of production or enterprise from collective control (national or cosmopolitan) increases the possible functions of money and so makes a different thing of it. Thus there can be endless species of money - as many types of money as there are types and varieties of social order. Money in Soviet Russia is a different organ from money French or American money. The difference can be as wide as that between lungs and swimming bladders and gills. It is not simply a quantitative difference, as so many people seem to imagine, which can be adjusted by varying the rate of exchange or any such contrivance, it goes deeper, it is a difference in quality and kind. The bare thought of that makes our business and financial people feel uncomfortable and confused and menaced, and they go on moving their bars of gold about from this vault to that, hoping almost beyond hope

131

that no one will say anything more about it. It worked very well for a time, to go on as though money was the same thing all the world over. They will not admit how that assumption is failing to work now.

Clever people reaped a certain advantage from a more or less definite apprehension of the variable nature of money, but since one could not be a financier or business director without an underlying faith in one's right to profit by one's superior cleverness, there did not seem to be any reason for them to make a public fuss about it. They got their profits and the flats got left.

Directly we grasp this not very obscure truth that there can be, and are, different sorts of money dependent on the economic usages or system in operation, which are not really interchangeable, then it becomes plain that a collectivist world order, whose fundamental law is such a Declaration of Rights as we have sketched, will have to carry on its main, its primary operations at least with a new world money, a specially contrived money, differing in its nature from any sort of money conventions that have hitherto served human needs. It will be issued against the total purchasable output of the community in return for the workers' services to the community. There will be no more reason for going to the City for a loan than for going to the oracle at Delphi for advice about it.

In the phase of social stress and emergency socialisation into which we are certainly passing, such a new money may begin to appear quite soon. Governments finding it impossible to resort to the tangled expedients of the financial counting-house, may take a short cut to recuperation, requisition the national resources within their reach and set their unemployment hands to work by means of these new checks. They may carry out international barter arrangements upon an increasing scale. The fact that the counting-house is in a hopeless mess because of its desperate attempts to ignore the protean nature of money, will become more manifest as it becomes less important.

The Stock Exchange and Bank credit and all arts of loaning and usury and forestalling will certainly dwindle away together as the World Order establishes itself. If and when World Order establishes itself. They will be superseded, like egg-shells and fœtal membranes. There is no reason for denouncing those who devised and worked those methods and institutions as scoundrels and villains. They did honestly according to their lights. They were a necessary part of the process of getting Homo sapiens out of his cave and down from his tree. And gold, that lovely heavy stuff, will be released from its vaults and hiding-places for the use of the artist and technician - probably at a price considerably below the present quotations.

Our attempt to forecast the coming World Order is framed then in an immense and increasing spectacle of constructive activity. We can anticipate a rapid transfiguration of the face of the earth as its population is distributed and re-distributed in accordance with the shifting requirements of economic production.

It is not only that there is what is called a housing shortage in nearly every region of the earth, but most of the existing accommodation, by modern standards, is unfit for human occupation. There is scarcely a city in the world, the new world as well as the old, which does not need to have half its dwelling-places destroyed. Perhaps Stockholm, reconditioned under a Socialist regime, may claim to be an exception; Vienna was doing hopefully until its spirit was broken by Dollfuss and the Catholic reaction. For the rest, behind a few hundred main avenues and prospects, sea and river fronts, capitols, castles and the like, filthy slums and rookeries cripple childhood and degrade and devitalise its dulled elders. You can hardly say people are born into such surroundings; they are only half born.

With the co-operation of the press and the cinema it would be easy to engender a world-wide public interest and enthusiasm for the new types of home and fitment that are now attainable by everyone. Here would be an outlet for urban and regional patriotism, for local shame and pride and effort. Here would be stuff to argue about. Wherever men and women have been rich enough, powerful enough and free enough, their thoughts have turned to architecture and gardening. Here would be a new incentive to travel, to see what other towns and country-sides were doing. The common man on his holidays would do what the English milord of the seventeenth century did; he would make his Grand Tour and come back from his journeys with architectural drawings and notions for home application. And this building and rebuilding would be a continuing process, a sustained employment, going on from good to better, as the economic forces shifted and changed with new discoveries and men's ideas expanded.

It is doubtful in a world of rising needs and standards if many people would want to live in manifestly old houses, any more than they would want to live in old clothes. Except in a few country places where ancient buildings have wedded themselves happily to some local loveliness and become quasi-natural things, or where some great city has shown a brave facade to the world, I doubt if there will be much to preserve. In such large open countries as the United States there has been a considerable development of the mobile home in recent years. People haul a trailer-home behind their cars and become seasonal nomads. . . . But there is no need to expatiate further on a limitless wealth of possibilities. Thousands of those who have been assisting in the monstrous clumsy evacuations and shiftings of population that have been going on recently, must have had their imaginations stirred by dim realisation of how much better all this might be done, if it were done in a new spirit and with a different intention. There must be a multitude of young and youngish people quite ripe for infection by this idea of cleaning up and resettling the world. Young men who are now poring over war maps and planning annexations and strategic boundaries, fresh Maginot lines, new Gibraltars and Dardanelles, may presently be scheming the happy and healthy distribution of routes and residential districts in relation to this or that important region of world supply for oil or wheat or water-power. It is essentially the same type of cerebration, better employed.

Considerations of this sort are sufficient to supply a background of hopeful activities to our prospective world order. But we are not all architects and gardeners there are many types of minds and many of those who are training or being trained for the skilled co-operations of warfare and the development of a combatant morale, may be more disposed to go on with definitely educational work. In that way they can most easily gratify the craving for power and honourable service. They will face a world in extreme need of more teachers and fresh-minded and inspiring teachers at that. At every level of educational work from the kindergarten to the research laboratory, and in every part of the world from Capricornia to Alaska and from the Gold Coast to Japan, there will be need of active workers to bring minds into harmony

135

with new order and to work out, with all the labour saving and multiplying apparatus available, cinema, radio, cheap books and pictures and all the rest of it, the endless new problems of human liaison that will arise. There we have a second line of work along which millions of young people may escape the stagnation and frustration which closed in upon their predecessors as the old order drew to its end.

A sturdy and assertive variety of the new young will be needed for the police work of the world. They will be more disposed for authority and less teaching or creative activities than their fellows. The old proverb will still hold for the new order that it takes all sorts to make a world, and the alternative to driving this type of temperament into conspiracy and fighting it and, if you can, suppressing it, is to employ it, win it over, trust it, and give it law behind it to respect and enforce. They want a loyalty and this loyalty will find its best use and satisfaction in the service of world order. I have remarked in the course of such air travel as I have done, that the airmen of all nations have a common resemblance to each other and that the patriotic virus in their blood is largely corrected by a wider professionalism. At present the outlook before a young airmen is to perish in a spectacular dog-fight before he is five and twenty. I wonder how many of them really rejoice in that prospect.

It is not unreasonable to anticipate the development of an ad hoc disarmament police which will have its greatest strength in the air. How easily the spirit of an air police can be de-nationalised is shown by the instance of the air patrols on the United States-Canadian border, to which President Roosevelt drew my attention. There is a lot of smuggling along that border and the planes now play an important part in its suppression. At first the United States and Canada had each their own planes. Then in a wave of common sense, the two services were pooled. Each plane now carries a United States and Canadian customs officer. When contraband is spotted the plane comes down on it and which officer acts is determined by the destination of the smuggled goods. There we have a pattern for a world struggling through federation to collective unity. An ad hoc disarmament police with its main strength in the air would necessarily fall into close co-operation with the various other world police activities. In a world where criminals can fly anywhere, the police must be able to fly anywhere too. Already we have a world-wide network of competent men fighting the white-slave traffic, the drug traffic and so forth. The thing begins already.

All this I write to provide imaginative material for those who see the coming order as a mere blank interrogation. People talk much nonsense about the disappearance of incentive under socialism. The exact opposite is the truth. It is the obstructive appropriation of natural resources by private ownership that robs the prosperous of incentive and the poor of hope. Our Declaration of Human rights assures a man the proper satisfaction of all his elementary needs in kind, and nothing more. If he wants more than that he will have to work for it, and the healthier he is and the better he is fed and housed, the more bored he will be by inactivity and the more he will want something to do. I am suggesting what he is likely to do in general terms, and that is as much as one can do now. We can talk about the broad principles upon which these matters will be handled in a consolidating world socialism, but we can scarcely venture to anticipate the detailed forms, the immense richness and variety of expression, an ever-increasing number of intelligent people will impose upon these primary ideas.

But there is one more structural suggestion that it may be necessary to bring into our picture. So far as I know it was first broached by that very bold and subtle thinker, Professor William James, in a small book entitled The Moral Equivalent of War. He pointed out the need there might be for a conception of duty, side by side with the idea of rights, that there should be something in the life of every citizen, man or woman alike, that should give him at once a sense of personal obligation to the World State. He brought that into relation with the fact that there will remain in any social order we can conceive, a multitude of necessary services which by no sort of device can be made attractive as normal life-long occupations. He was not thinking so much of the fast-vanishing problem of mechanical toil as the such irksome tasks as the prison warder's, the asylum attendant's; the care of the aged and infirm, nursing generally, health and sanitary services, a certain residuum of clerical routine, dangerous exploration and experiment. No doubt human goodness is sufficient to supply volunteers for many of these things, but are the rest of us entitled to profit by their devotion? His solution is universal conscription for a certain period of the adult life. The young will have to do so much service and take so much risk for the general welfare as the world commonwealth requires. They will be able to do these jobs with the freshness and vigour of those who know they will presently be released, and who find their honour through performance; they will not be subjected to that deadening temptation to self-protective slacking and mechanical insensitiveness, which assails all who are thrust by economic necessity into these callings for good and all.

It is quite possible that a certain percentage of these conscripts may be caught by the interest of what they are doing; the

asylum attendant may decide to specialise in psycho-
therapeutic work; the hospital nurse succumb to that curiosity
which underlies the great physiologist; the Arctic worker may
fall in love with his snowy wilderness. . . .

One other leading probability of a collectivist world order has
to be noted here, and that is an enormous increase in the pace
and amount of research and discovery. I write research, but by
that I mean that double-barrelled attack upon ignorance, the
biological attack and the physical attack, that is generally
known as "Science". "Science" comes to us from those
academic Dark Ages when men had to console themselves for
their ignorance by pretending that there was a limited amount
of knowledge in the world, and little chaps in caps and gowns
strutted about, bachelors who knew all that there was to be
known. Now it is manifest that none of us know very much,
and the more we look into what we think we know, the more
hitherto undetected things we shall find lurking in our
assumptions.

Hitherto this business of research, which we call the "scientific
world", has been in the hands of very few workers indeed. I
throw out the suggestion that in our present-day world, of all
the brains capable of great and masterful contributions to
"scientific" thought and achievement, brains of the quality of
Lord Rutherford's, or Darwin's or Mendel's or Freud's or
Leonardo's or Galileo's, not one in a thousand, not one in a
score of thousands, ever gets born into such conditions as to
realise its opportunities. The rest never learn a civilised
language, never get near a library, never have the faintest
chance of self-realisation, never hear the call. They are under-
nourished, they die young, they are misused. And of the

139

millions who would make good, useful, eager secondary research workers and explorers, not one in a million is utilised.

But now consider how things will be if we had a stirring education ventilating the whole world, and if we had a systematic and continually more competent search for exceptional mental quality and a continually more extensive net of opportunity for it. Suppose a quickening public mind implies an atmosphere of increasing respect for intellectual achievement and livelier criticism of imposture. What we call scientific progress to-day would seem a poor, hesitating, uncertain advance in comparison with what would be happening under these happier conditions.

The progress of research and discovery has produced such brilliant and startling results in the past century and a half that few of us are aware of the small number of outstanding men who have been concerned in it, and how the minor figures behind these leaders trail off into a following of timid and ill-provided specialists who dare scarcely stand up to a public official on their own ground. This little army, this "scientific world" of to-day, numbering I suppose from head to tail, down to the last bottle-washer, not a couple of hundred thousand men, will certainly be represented in the new world order by a force of millions, better equipped, amply co-ordinated, free to question, able to demand opportunity. Its best will be no better than our best, who could not be better, but they will be far more numerous, and its rank and file, explorers, prospectors, experimental team workers and an encyclopædic host of classifiers and co-ordinators and interpreters, will have a vigour, a pride and confidence that will make the laboratories of to-day seem half-way back to the alchemist's den.

Can one doubt that the "scientific world" will break out in this way when the revolution is achieved, and that the development of man's power over nature and over his own nature and over this still unexplored planet, will undergo a continual acceleration as the years pass? No man can guess beforehand what doors will open then nor upon what wonderlands.

These are some fragmentary intimations of the quality of that wider life a new world order can open to mankind. I will not speculate further about them because I would not have it said that this book is Utopian or "Imaginative" or anything of that sort. I have set down nothing that is not strictly reasonable and practicable. It is the soberest of books and the least original of books. I think I have written enough to show that it is impossible for world affairs to remain at their present level. Either mankind collapses or our species struggles up by the hard yet fairly obvious routes I have collated in this book, to reach a new level of social organisation. There can be little question of the abundance, excitement and vigour of living that awaits our children upon that upland. If it is attained. There is no doubting their degradation and misery if it is not.

There is nothing really novel about this book. But there has been a certain temerity in bringing together facts that many people have avoided bringing together for fear they might form an explosive mixture. Maybe they will. They may blast through some obstinate mental barriers. In spite of that explosive possibility, that explosive necessity, it may be this remains essentially an assemblage, digest and encouragement of now prevalent but still hesitating ideas. It is a plain statement of the revolution to which reason points an increasing number of minds, but which they still lack resolution to undertake. In The Fate of Homo sapiens I have stressed the urgency of the case. Here I have assembled the things they can and need to do. They had better summon up their resolution.

CPSIA information can be obtained at www.ICGtesting.com
Printed in the USA
BVOW05s0706120314

347409BV00010B/339/P